opta

World Football Infographics

PUBLISHER'S NOTES

All European domestic league infographic data runs up until the end of the 2016–17 season.
All European team names printed in accordance with UEFA.

First published in Great Britain in 2016 by
Carlton Books Limited
20 Mortimer Street
London W1T 3JW

Second Edition 2017

Infographic statistical data © Perform Media Channels Limited 2016, 2017

All other text, graphics and design © Carlton Books Limited 2016, 2017

A CIP catalogue record for this book is available from the British Library

Editorial Manager: Martin Corteel
Design Manager: Luke Griffin
Editorial Assistant: Malcolm Croft
Text: Adrian Besley
Opta Data: Duncan Alexander and Tom Ede
Picture Research: Paul Langan
Production: Lisa Cook
Infographics and Visualisation: Visual Evolution and James Pople

ISBN 978-1-78097-995-3

Printed in Dubai

opta

World Football Infographics

The Beautiful Game in Revelatory Detail

Trends, Statistics and Data Analysis

SECOND EDITION

CARLTON
BOOKS

WORLD CUP

EUROPE

NORTH & CENTRAL AMERICA

CONCACAF GOLD CUP

MLS

SOUTH AMERICA

COPA AMÉRICA

COPA LIBERTADORES

AFRICA

AFRICA CUP OF NATIONS

ASIA

AFC ASIAN CUP

MISCELLANEOUS

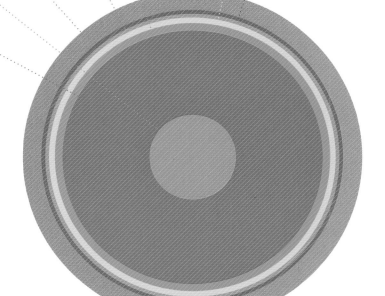

opta

Foreword

It is now 20 years since Opta started collecting football data and in that time the popularity of the information produced has gone from being a curiosity in a newspaper or TV feature to an integral part of sports coverage in every type of media.

Data was long seen as the preserve of the anorak, only accessible to those willing to pore through statistical tomes to find "interesting" snippets of information. Today it's consumed by ordinary football fans through a variety of methods. You'll still see tables of numbers and hear facts and figures spoken by commentators, pundits or by people to their friends on their way to matches, but you're now just as likely to see a graphical interpretation of that information.

From pie charts and bar charts, to radars and word clouds, numbers are regularly turned into easily understandable graphics, where the viewer can see what you're trying to tell them instantly. Added to that, the positional and tracking data available within sport allows tactical insight to be communicated easily through heat maps, average formation graphics or expected goals visualizations, which show at a glance the chance of scoring from a particular position on the pitch relative to other types of shots.

Infographics have become one of the most quickly developing trends in sports data analysis. As datasets become more complex, infographics are an invaluable way of displaying complex information in a clear, concise, attractive way. The unique infographics created for the second edition of this book, incorporating comparisons between players, teams and leagues for almost every continent, showcases the mass of detailed data now available from right across the world of football.

Enjoy the book

Rob Bateman (@Orbinho)

Introduction

Statistics are an integral part of modern football – pored over by coaches, analysts and armchair fans alike. Rarely though, have the thrills and skills, triumphs and trophies of the global game been transformed into such thought-provoking graphs, diagrams and charts as those presented on the pages that follow. You'll be amazed at what emerges from these technicolour infographics. From the statistics that illuminate the Messi–Ronaldo rivalry to the evolution of team formations, right through to the different parts of the body used to score World Cup goals – it's all here… and more.

Our fascination with football takes many forms. We can admire the breathtaking skills of stars such as Mesut Özil, Eden Hazard or Neymar; the performances of great teams like Bayern München and Real Madrid and the strategies of coaches such as José Mourinho and Antonio Conte. However, in recent years, statistics, trends and data collection have added to our interest of top-level football. And, where there are numbers, there can be infographics capable of unlocking the power of big data and presenting it in a brilliant, captivating way.

This invaluable book uses imaginative infographics to take a topical look at the trends and data in top-class football. It compares the top leagues and players across Europe and assesses the performances in the Champions League, Europa League and Copa Libertadores. At international level, we see the domination and surprises of the nation's tournaments around the world. And, of course, the greatest footballing show on earth, the FIFA World Cup, is represented in vibrant infographics that include analysis on goalkeepers, goal recreations and perfect penalty placements. Intriguing charts and maps also reveal other footballing facets such as club rivalries, stadium sizes, MLS in the United States, the FIFA World Player of the Year and where to find the most shots from distance or dribbles.

Thanks to the rich and compelling information supplied by data providers such as Opta, football is no longer just a simple game of two halves. The doors have been blown open and the beautiful game is just that little bit more beautiful.

1966 WORLD CUP GOALS

Many nations fancied their chances of winning the World Cup in 1966: West Germany, Argentina, Brazil and England were all confident it would be their turn to lift the Jules Rimet trophy. Despite being blighted by the barbaric treatment of Pelé and some controversial refereeing, the tournament was enlightened by the giant-slaying North Korea, the brilliance of Eusébio and a nail-biting, but triumphant, final for the host nation. The 1966 World Cup also saw goals that would become legendary, including the lung-bursting run from West Germany's Franz Beckenbauer, an outside-of-the-foot free kick from Brazil's Garrincha and Geoff Hurst's monumental hat-trick in the final – the first ever in a World Cup final.

GEOFF HURST – England vs West Germany

England's Geoff Hurst scores that famous fourth goal to put England 4–2 up against West Germany after extra time, 30 July 1966.

1. Pass (chipped, cross) **Schulz**
2. Ball recovery **Moore**
3. Pass **Moore**
4. Pass **Hunt**
5. Pass (chipped, long ball) **Moore**
6. Goal **Hurst**

KEY

Ball movement	———	Player with ball ··········
Shot	———⚽	Player without ball ··········

LUIS ARTIME – Argentina vs Spain

1. Interception **Más**
2. Pass **Más**
3. Pass **Solari**
4. Pass **Rattín**
5. Pass **Onega**
6. Pass **Solari**
7. Goal **Artime**

FRANZ BECKENBAUER – West Germany vs Switzerland

JÁNOS FARKAS – Hungary vs Brazil

1. Pass **Gérson**
2. Pass **Mátrai**
3. Pass **Mészöly**
4. Pass **Káposzta**
5. Pass **Albert**
6. Pass (cross, chipped, long ball) **Bene**
7. Goal **Farkas**

EDUARD MALOFEYEV – USSR vs DPR Korea

PREMIER LEAGUE FOULS AND CARDS

The number of bookings and dismissals has been gradually increasing since the Premier League began in 1992. Although referee clampdowns and new rules to protect players from reckless challenges have increased the tally, statistics reveal a large number of indiscretions are due to rash decisions and second offences. It appears that as the game gets quicker, and more skilful, tackling becomes a much riskier business. So, hats off to Ryan Giggs. He managed 632 Premier League appearances without seeing red once.

CHELSEA 1536

EVERTON 1465

ARSENAL 1417

TOTTENHAM HOTSPUR 1397

ASTON VILLA 1362

MANCHESTER UNITED 1336

WEST HAM UNITED 1321

LIVERPOOL 1220

NEWCASTLE UNITED 1220

MANCHESTER CITY 1158

BLACKBURN ROVERS 1111

SUNDERLAND 1095

SOUTHAMPTON 996

MIDDLESBROUGH 973

BOLTON WANDERERS 845

LEEDS UNITED 790

FULHAM 708

WEST BROMWICH ALBION 645

LEICESTER CITY 619

STOKE CITY 617

DERBY COUNTY 538

WIGAN ATHLETIC 513

COVENTRY CITY 481

CRYSTAL PALACE 477

BIRMINGHAM CITY 428

CHARLTON ATHLETIC 408

WIMBLEDON 407

PORTSMOUTH 398

NORWICH CITY 394

QUEENS PARK RANGERS 364

SHEFFIELD WEDNESDAY 341

HULL CITY 328

SWANSEA CITY 318

NOTTINGHAM FOREST 287

WATFORD 272

WOLVERHAMPTON WANDERERS 255

BURNLEY 186

IPSWICH TOWN 183

SHEFFIELD UNITED 170

READING 142

BRADFORD CITY 113

BOURNEMOUTH 105

OLDHAM ATHLETIC 70

BARNSLEY 66

CARDIFF CITY 50

BLACKPOOL 47

SWINDON TOWN 39

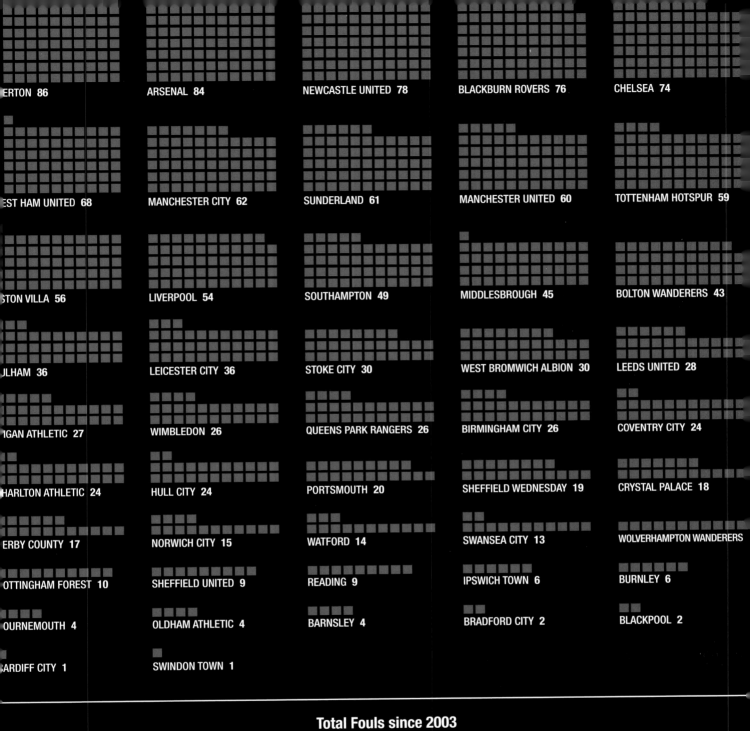

ERTON 86

ARSENAL 84

NEWCASTLE UNITED 78

BLACKBURN ROVERS 76

CHELSEA 74

EST HAM UNITED 68

MANCHESTER CITY 62

SUNDERLAND 61

MANCHESTER UNITED 60

TOTTENHAM HOTSPUR 59

STON VILLA 56

LIVERPOOL 54

SOUTHAMPTON 49

MIDDLESBROUGH 45

BOLTON WANDERERS 43

JLHAM 36

LEICESTER CITY 36

STOKE CITY 30

WEST BROMWICH ALBION 30

LEEDS UNITED 28

IGAN ATHLETIC 27

WIMBLEDON 26

QUEENS PARK RANGERS 26

BIRMINGHAM CITY 26

COVENTRY CITY 24

HARLTON ATHLETIC 24

HULL CITY 24

PORTSMOUTH 20

SHEFFIELD WEDNESDAY 19

CRYSTAL PALACE 18

ERBY COUNTY 17

NORWICH CITY 15

WATFORD 14

SWANSEA CITY 13

WOLVERHAMPTON WANDERERS

OTTINGHAM FOREST 10

SHEFFIELD UNITED 9

READING 9

IPSWICH TOWN 6

BURNLEY 6

OURNEMOUTH 4

OLDHAM ATHLETIC 4

BARNSLEY 4

BRADFORD CITY 2

BLACKPOOL 2

ARDIFF CITY 1

SWINDON TOWN 1

Total Fouls since 2003

EVERTON **6679**
ASTON VILLA **6576**
MANCHESTER CITY **6536**
CHELSEA **6274**
MANCHESTER UNITED **6270**
TOTTENHAM HOTSPUR **6259**
LIVERPOOL **6151**
ARSENAL **5988**
NEWCASTLE UNITED **5771**
WEST HAM UNITED **5292**

FULHAM **5233**
SUNDERLAND **5105**
BLACKBURN ROVERS **5044**
BOLTON WANDERERS **4871**
WEST BROMWICH ALBION **4521**
STOKE CITY **4222**
WIGAN ATHLETIC **4042**
PORTSMOUTH **3728**
MIDDLESBROUGH **3648**
SOUTHAMPTON **3214**

BIRMINGHAM CITY **3085**
CRYSTAL PALACE **2440**
HULL CITY **2398**
SWANSEA CITY **2295**
NORWICH CITY **2254**
CHARLTON ATHLETIC **2013**
WOLVERHAMPTON WANDERERS **1901**
LEICESTER CITY **1883**
WATFORD **1573**
READING **1341**

BURNLEY **1296**
QUEENS PARK RANGERS **1262**
BOURNEMOUTH **729**
LEEDS UNITED **583**
DERBY COUNTY **548**
SHEFFIELD UNITED **510**
BLACKPOOL **440**
CARDIFF CITY **345**

AFRICA CUP OF NATIONS TROPHIES AND GOALS

What began in 1957 with a three-team competition has developed 31 tournaments later into a month-long, 16-team extravaganza. The tournament has witnessed many great moments, including Benni McCarthy hitting four goals in 13 minutes against Namibia in 1998; Ivory Coast's second-choice keeper Boubacar Barry saving two penalties before hitting the winner in the shoot-out in 2015 and Vincent Aboubakar's sensational 88th minute strike to win the trophy for Cameroon in 2017.

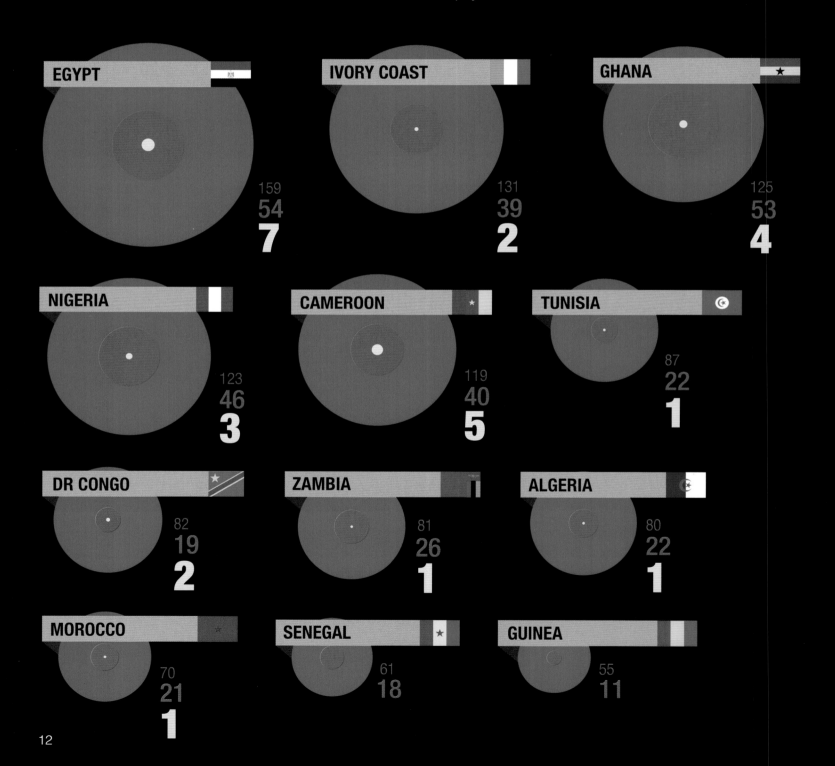

EGYPT
159
54
7

IVORY COAST
131
39
2

GHANA
125
53
4

NIGERIA
123
46
3

CAMEROON
119
40
5

TUNISIA
87
22
1

DR CONGO
82
19
2

ZAMBIA
81
26
1

ALGERIA
80
22
1

MOROCCO
70
21
1

SENEGAL
61
18

GUINEA
55
11

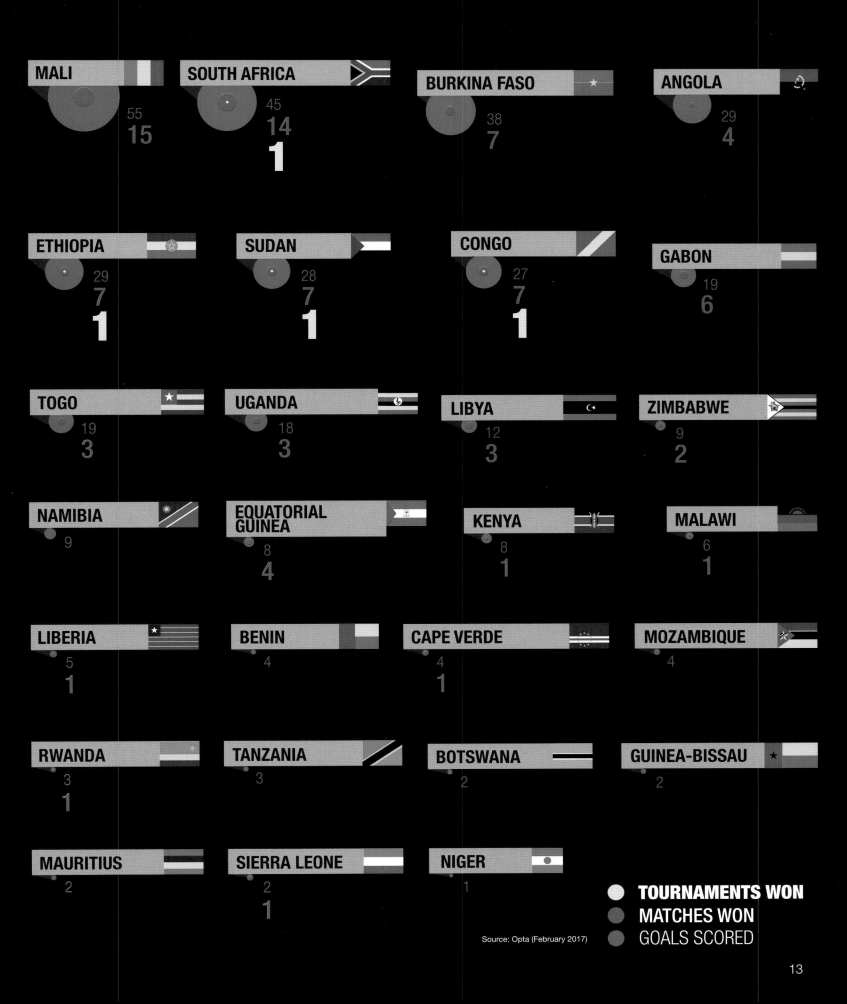

MALI
55
15

SOUTH AFRICA
45
14
1

BURKINA FASO
38
7

ANGOLA
29
4

ETHIOPIA
29
7
1

SUDAN
28
7
1

CONGO
27
7
1

GABON
19
6

TOGO
19
3

UGANDA
18
3

LIBYA
12
3

ZIMBABWE
9
2

NAMIBIA
9

EQUATORIAL GUINEA
8
4

KENYA
8
1

MALAWI
6
1

LIBERIA
5
1

BENIN
4

CAPE VERDE
4
1

MOZAMBIQUE
4

RWANDA
3
1

TANZANIA
3

BOTSWANA
2

GUINEA-BISSAU
2

MAURITIUS
2

SIERRA LEONE
2
1

NIGER
1

● TOURNAMENTS WON
● MATCHES WON
● GOALS SCORED

Source: Opta (February 2017)

13

WORLD CUP FINALS RESULTS 1930–2014

The FIFA World Cup has grown from a small tournament comprising 13 teams from Europe and South America (USA and Mexico participated too) to 32 nations from five continents battling it out in the most widely followed sporting event in the world. There have been 20 to date, each one as spectacular as the last. Every tournament has had its amazing stories, controversies, moments that took our breath away and heartbreak that saw us plunge into despair. Behind all these iconic events, what remains (apart from memories) are these simple facts – the statistics that mark each country's triumphs and disappointments in black and white. Make of these what you will...

Source: Google (October 2015)

1930	1934
4 Uruguay vs Argentina 2	2 Italy vs Czechoslovakia 1

1938	1950
4 Italy vs Hungary 2	2 Uruguay vs Brazil 1

1954	1958
3 West Germany vs Hungary 2	5 Brazil vs Sweden 2

1962	1966
3 Brazil vs Czechoslovakia 1	4 England vs West Germany 2

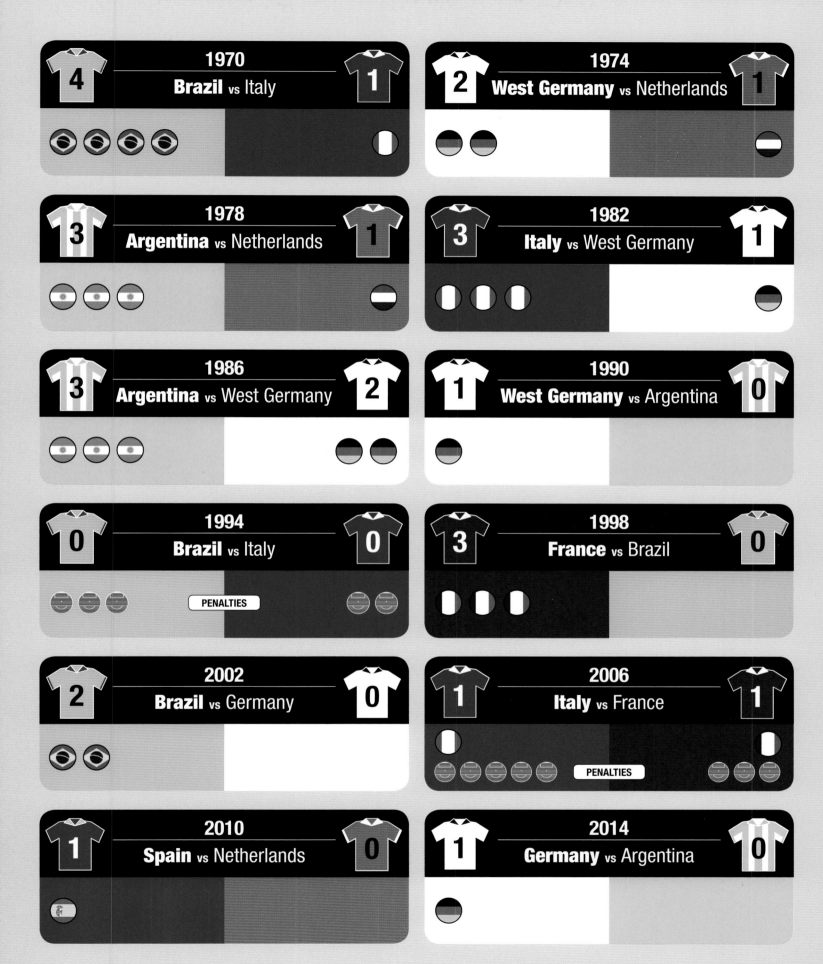

1970 Brazil vs Italy — 4 : 1

1974 West Germany vs Netherlands — 2 : 1

1978 Argentina vs Netherlands — 3 : 1

1982 Italy vs West Germany — 3 : 1

1986 Argentina vs West Germany — 3 : 2

1990 West Germany vs Argentina — 1 : 0

1994 Brazil vs Italy — 0 : 0 PENALTIES

1998 France vs Brazil — 3 : 0

2002 Brazil vs Germany — 2 : 0

2006 Italy vs France — 1 : 1 PENALTIES

2010 Spain vs Netherlands — 1 : 0

2014 Germany vs Argentina — 1 : 0

EREDIVISIE TITLE WINNERS

The Eredivisie, the top league of the Netherlands, was founded in 1956, two years after the start of professional football in the country. It is placed 13th in UEFA's ranking of European leagues. The Dutch league has been dominated by three teams, all ever-presents in the league: Ajax (24 titles), PSV Eindhoven (18) and Feyenoord (10), whose 2017 success was their first for 18 years. Only AZ Alkmaar and FC Twente have managed to break the grip of the "Big Three" this century.

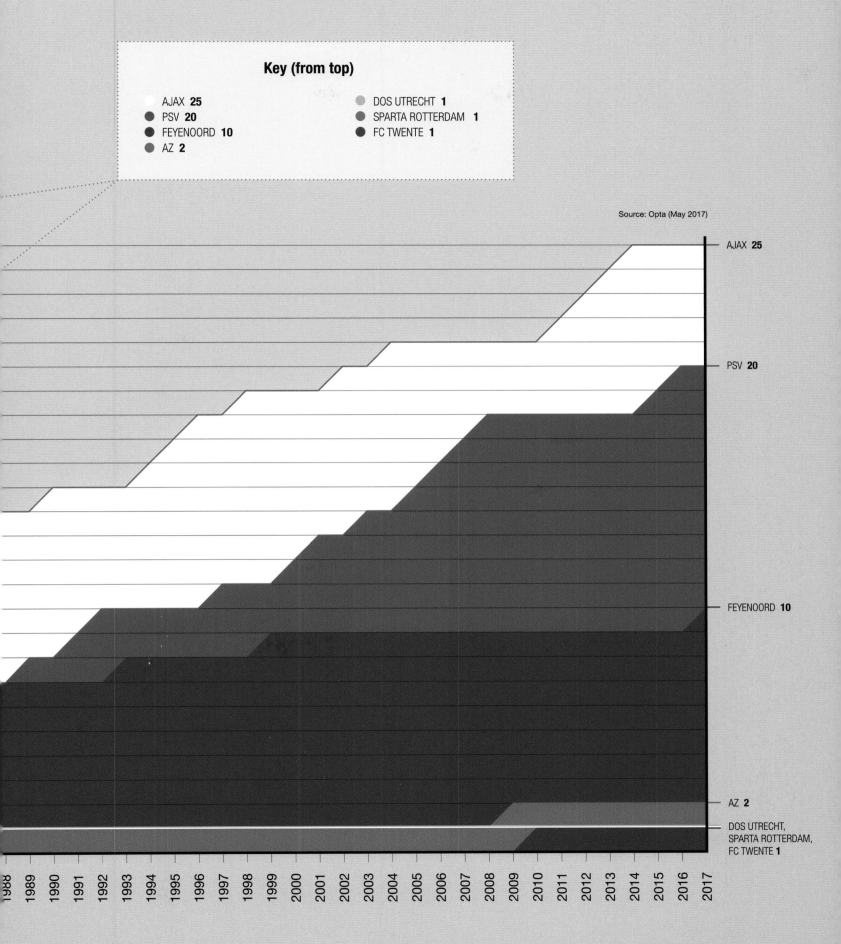

Key (from top)

● AJAX **25**
● PSV **20**
● FEYENOORD **10**
● AZ **2**

● DOS UTRECHT **1**
● SPARTA ROTTERDAM **1**
● FC TWENTE **1**

Source: Opta (May 2017)

AJAX **25**

PSV **20**

FEYENOORD **10**

AZ **2**

DOS UTRECHT,
SPARTA ROTTERDAM,
FC TWENTE **1**

1988 1989 1990 1991 1992 1993 1994 1995 1996 1997 1998 1999 2000 2001 2002 2003 2004 2005 2006 2007 2008 2009 2010 2011 2012 2013 2014 2015 2016 2017

EUROPEAN CHAMPIONSHIP RECORDS BY NATION

Brainchild of Henri Delaunay, the secretary of the French Football Federation, the European Championship has been held every four years since 1960. Qualification for the first two finals was conducted on a home-and-away knockout basis, with the group qualification format beginning in 1968. Originally only four teams qualified for the finals. This was extended to eight teams in 1980, to 16 from 1996 and further expanded to include 24 nations in 2016. To mark 60 years of the tournament, the 2020 finals will be held in 13 different cities across the continent.

Iceland

Norway

Sweden

Scotland

Denmark

Northern Ireland

Netherlands

Republic of Ireland

Wales

Germany

England

Belgium

Czech Republic

Austria

France

Switzerland

Slovenia

Croatia

Spain

Portugal

Italy

QUALIFICATION NOTES
Germany: Five qualifications as West Germany.
Serbia: Four qualifications as Yugoslavia.
Russia: Five qualifications as USSR and one as CIS.
Czech Republic: Three qualifications as Czechoslovakia.

COUNTRY NOTES
USSR (1960) and Czechoslovakia (1976) won the championship once.
West Germany won the championship twice in 1972 and 1980.
Yugoslavia (1976) and West Germany (1988) hosted the championship once.

Source: UEFA: July 2016

18

FOOTBALL RIVALRIES: PART 1

History, tradition, passion and pride – these are the elements that come to the fore when great footballing rivals collide. Every nation has its rival teams. Some, such as Tottenham Hotspur and Arsenal, are born from geographical proximity – they're based four miles apart. France's Olympique de Marseille and Paris Saint-Germain may reside further apart, but the rivalry between the North and South, and the country's two biggest cities, makes the "Le Classique" derby just as bitterly fought.

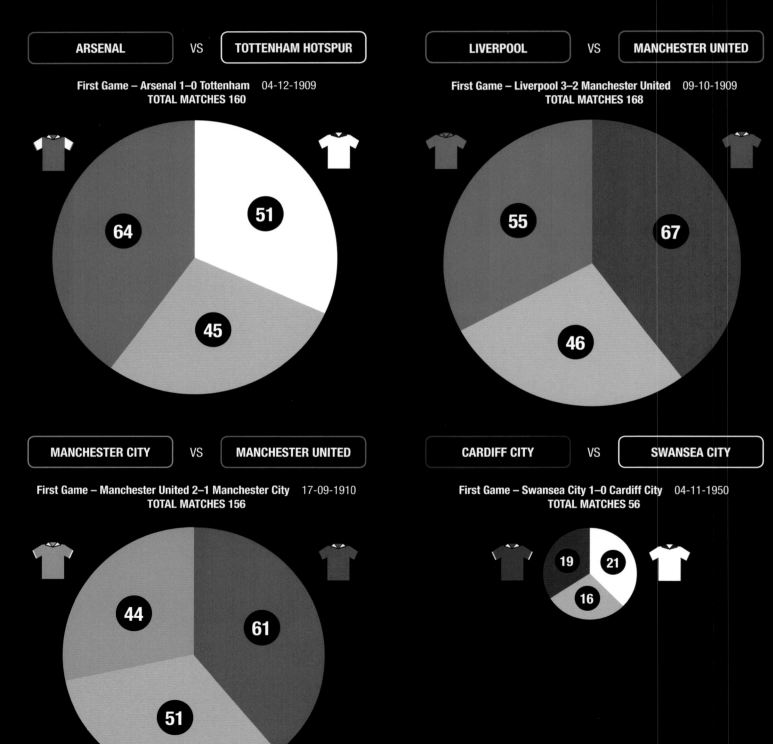

ARSENAL VS **TOTTENHAM HOTSPUR**

First Game – Arsenal 1–0 Tottenham   04-12-1909
TOTAL MATCHES 160

64   51   45

LIVERPOOL VS **MANCHESTER UNITED**

First Game – Liverpool 3–2 Manchester United   09-10-1909
TOTAL MATCHES 168

55   67   46

MANCHESTER CITY VS **MANCHESTER UNITED**

First Game – Manchester United 2–1 Manchester City   17-09-1910
TOTAL MATCHES 156

44   61   51

CARDIFF CITY VS **SWANSEA CITY**

First Game – Swansea City 1–0 Cardiff City   04-11-1950
TOTAL MATCHES 56

19   21   16

| **HAMBURGER SV** | VS | **BAYERN MÜNCHEN** |

First Game – Hamburger SV 0–4 Bayern München   20-10-1965
TOTAL MATCHES 104

| **BAYERN MÜNCHEN** | VS | **BORUSSIA DORTMUND** |

First Game – Borussia Dortmund 2–0 Bayern München   16-10-1965
TOTAL MATCHES 96

| **OLYMPIQUE DE MARSEILLE** | VS | **SAINT-ÉTIENNE** |

First Game – Saint-Étienne 1–0 Olympique de Marseille   06-11-1938
TOTAL MATCHES 104

| **OLYMPIQUE LYONNAIS** | VS | **OLYMPIQUE DE MARSEILLE** |

First Game – Olympique Lyonnais 2–2 Olympique de Marseille   11-11-1951
TOTAL MATCHES 94

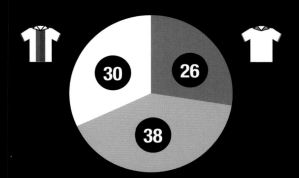

| **OLYMPIQUE DE MARSEILLE** | VS | **PARIS SAINT-GERMAIN** |

First Game – Olympique de Marseille 4–2 Paris Saint-Germain   12-12-1971
TOTAL MATCHES 76

"On derby day in Manchester the city is cut in two. The Blues and the Reds invade the street and if your team wins the city belongs to you."

Eric Cantona

Source: Opta (May 2017)

EUROPEAN ATTENDANCES

Attendances in the top tiers of European football average around 30,000 per game, with the Bundesliga and the Premier League attracting the highest average crowds. Despite rising ticket prices and more televised games, the gates in England, Germany and Spain continue to rise, while those in Italy and France remain static. Over the next few years major new stadia and expansions by clubs who already sell out many games, including Tottenham Hotspur, Atlético Madrid, Barcelona, Valencia and Liverpool, could see further sharp rises in attendances.

Source: Opta (May 2017)

KEY:

STADIUM CAPACITY

AVERAGE ATTENDANCE

x

RANKING OF STADIUM IN LEAGUE (CAPACITY)

ENGLISH PREMIER LEAGUE

95%

AVERAGE CAPACITY: 37786
AVERAGE ATTENDANCE: 35822

1 · **Manchester United** · Old Trafford · 75,731 · **75,290**
2 · **Arsenal FC** · Emirates Stadium · 60,362 · **59,957**
3 · **West Ham United** · London Stadium · 60,000 · **56,972**
4 · **Manchester City** · Etihad Stadium · 55,097 · **54,019**
5 · **Liverpool FC** · Anfield · 54,074 · **53,016**
6 · **Sunderland AFC** · Stadium of Light · 49,000 · **41,287**
7 · **Chelsea FC** · Stamford Bridge · 41,837 · **41,508**
8 · **Everton FC** · Goodison Park · 40,157 · **39,310**
9 · **Tottenham Hotspur** · White Hart Lane · 36,284 · **31,639**
10 · **Middlesbrough FC** · Riverside · 35,100 · **30,449**
11 · **Southampton FC** · Saint Mary's · 32,689 · **30,936**
12 · **Leicester City** · King Power Stadium · 32,500 · **31,893**
13 · **Stoke City** · bet365 Stadium · 27,740 · **27,433**
14 · **West Bromwich Albion** · The Hawthorns · 26,445 · **23,876**
15 · **Crystal Palace** · Selhurst Park · 26,255 · **25,161**
16 · **Hull City** · Kingston Communications Stadium · 25,586 · **20,761**
17 · **Burnley FC** · Turf Moor · 22,546 · **20,558**
18 · **Watford FC** · Vicarage Road · 22,100 · **20,571**
19 · **Swansea City** · Liberty Stadium · 20,750 · **20,619**
20 · **Bournemouth** · Vitality Stadium · 11,464 · **11,182**

GERMAN BUNDESLIGA

93%

AVERAGE CAPACITY: 40260
AVERAGE ATTENDANCE: 37367

1 · **Borussia Dortmund** · Signal Iduna Park · 81,359 · **79,653**
2 · **Bayern München** · Allianz Arena · 75,000 · **75,000**
3 · **Hertha BSC** · Olympiastadion · 74,400 · **50,267**
4 · **FC Schalke 04** · Veltins-Arena · 62,271 · **60,703**
5 · **Hamburger SV** · Volksparkstadion · 57,000 · **52,341**
6 · **Bor. Mönchengladbach** · Borussia-Park · 54,067 · **51,494**
7 · **Eintracht Frankfurt** · Commerzbank-Arena · 51,500 · **49,176**
8 · **1. FC Köln** · RheinEnergieStadion · 50,997 · **49,571**
9 · **RB Leipzig** · Red Bull Arena · 44,279 · **41,454**
10 · **Werder Bremen** · Weser-Stadion · 42,100 · **40,881**
11 · **1. FSV Mainz 05** · Opel Arena · 34,000 · **29,096**
12 · **FC Augsburg** · WWK ARENA · 30,660 · **28,172**
13 · **Bayer Leverkusen** · BayArena · 30,210 · **28,428**
14 · **1899 Hoffenheim** · Wirsol Rhein-Neckar-Arena · 30,150 · **28,155**
15 · **VfL Wolfsburg** · Volkswagen Arena · 30,000 · **27,586**
16 · **SC Freiburg** · Schwarzwald-Stadion · 24,000 · **23,959**
17 · **SV Darmstadt 98** · Jonathan-Heimes-Stadion am Böllenfalltor · 17,400 · **16,794**
18 · **FC Ingolstadt 04** · Audi Sportpark · 15,800 · **14,601**

SPANISH LA LIGA

71%

1 · **FC Barcelona** · Camp Nou · 99,354 · **77,904**
2 · **Real Madrid** · Santiago Bernabéu · 81,044 · **68,718**
3 · **Real Betis** · Benito Villamarín · 56,500 · **31,623**
4 · **Atlético Madrid** · Vicente Calderón · 54,851 · **44,675**
5 · **Athletic Bilbao** · San Mamés · 53,332 · **41,073**
6 · **Valencia CF** · Estadio de Mestalla · 52,600 · **33,920**
7 · **Sevilla FC** · Ramón Sánchez Pizjuán · 45,500 · **32,825**

8 · **Espanyol Barcelona** · RCDE Stadium · 40,500 · **20,171**
9 · **Deportivo La Coruña** · Riazor · 34,600 · **22,353**
10 · **Real Sociedad** · Anoeta · 32,076 · **21,430**
11 · **Celta Vigo** · Municipal de Balaídos · 31,800 · **16,649**
12 · **UD Las Palmas** · Estadio de Gran Canaria · 31,250 · **20,409**
13 · **Málaga CF** · La Rosaleda · 30,044 · **22,090**
14 · **Sporting Gijón** · El Molinón · 30,000 · **22,692**

15 · **Villarreal CF** · Estadio de la Cerámica · 24,500 · **17,545**
16 · **Granada CF** · Nuevo Los Cármenes · 22,500 · **14,969**
17 · **CD Alavés** · Mendizorroza · 19,840 · **16,464**
18 · **CA Osasuna** · El Sadar · 19,800 · **14,798**
19 · **CD Leganés** · Municipal de Butarque · 10,958 · **9,627**
20 · **SD Eibar** · Ipurua · 6,267 · **5,320**

AVERAGE CAPACITY: 38866
AVERAGE ATTENDANCE: 27763

CANARY ISLANDS

FRENCH LIGUE 1

64%

1 · **Olympique Marseille** · Vélodrome · 67,394 · **39,894**
2 · **Olympique Lyon** · Stade des Lumières · 59,500 · **39,171**
3 · **Lille OSC** · Stade Pierre Mauroy · 50,186 · **29,487**
4 · **Paris Saint-Germain** · Parc des Princes · 48,712 · **45,159**
5 · **Girondins Bordeaux** · Matmut Atlantique · 42,052 · **24,217**
6 · **FC Nantes** · La Beaujoire · 38,500 · **23,152**
7 · **OGC Nice** · Allianz Riviera · 35,624 · **22,949**
8 · **AS Saint-Étienne** · Geoffroy Guichard · 35,616 · **25,792**
9 · **Toulouse FC** · Stade Municipal · 35,575 · **17,068**
10 · **Montpellier HSC** · La Mosson · 32,950 · **12,356**

11 · **Stade Rennes** · Roazhon Park · 31,127 · **22,688**
12 · **FC Metz** · Municipal St.-Symphorien · 26,700 · **15,344**
13 · **SM Caen** · Michel-d'Ornano · 21,500 · **15,927**
14 · **AS Nancy** · Marcel Picot · 20,087 · **17,516**
15 · **AS Monaco** · Louis II · 18,524 · **9,104**
16 · **EA Guingamp** · Municipal du Roudourou · 18,016 · **14,790**
17 · **SC Bastia** · Armand Cesari · 17,000 · **8,726**
18 · **FC Lorient** · Stade du Mouchoir · 16,910 · **11,831**
19 · **Angers SCO** · Jean-Bouin · 16,300 · **11,953**
20 · **Dijon FCO** · Gaston-Gérard · 15,000 · **10,126**

AVERAGE CAPACITY: 32364
AVERAGE ATTENDANCE: 20863

ITALIAN SERIE A

54%

1 · **Inter** · Giuseppe Meazza · 80,018 · **46,620**
2 · **AC Milan** · Giuseppe Meazza · 80,018 · **40,294**
3 · **AS Roma** · Olimpico · 72,698 · **32,638**
4 · **Lazio Roma** · Olimpico · 72,698 · **21,953**
5 · **SSC Napoli** · San Paolo · 60,240 · **36,605**
6 · **ACF Fiorentina** · Artemio Franchi · 47,284 · **26,470**
7 · **Juventus** · Allianz Stadium · 41,254 · **39,500**
8 · **Chievo Verona** · Marc Antonio Bentegodi · 39,211 · **12,684**

9 · **Bologna FC** · Renato Dall'Ara · 38,375 · **21,189**
10 · **US Palermo** · Renzo Barbera · 37,000 · **13,204**
11 · **Genoa CFC** · Luigi Ferraris · 36,603 · **21,525**
12 · **Sampdoria** · Luigi Ferraris · 36,603 · **19,852**
13 · **Atalanta** · Atleti Azzurri d'Italia · 26,562 · **16,946**
14 · **Torino FC** · Olimpico · 25,370 · **18,120**
15 · **Udinese Calcio** · Dacia Arena · 25,144 · **17,448**
16 · **Pescara Calcio** · Stadio Adriatico · 20,515 · **13,540**

17 · **Sassuolo Calcio** · Mapei Stadium · 20,084 · **12,362**
18 · **Empoli FC** · Carlo Castellani · 19,847 · **9,483**
19 · **FC Crotone** · Ezio Scida · 16,547 · **8,226**
20 · **Cagliari Calcio** · Is Arenas · 16,200 · **13,021**

CORSICA

AVERAGE CAPACITY: 40614
AVERAGE ATTENDANCE: 22084

1970 WORLD CUP GOALS

Many pundits, players and fans still regard the 1970 World Cup in Mexico as the finest World Cup tournament of all. Reigning champions England played Brazil in a scintillating group game, Italy met Germany in the "Game of the Century" – Italy won 4–3 after five goals were scored in extra time, the only FIFA World Cup game when this has happened – and the final was a masterclass in demolition by the Brazilian squad. It was Carlos Alberto's perfect strike that was the nail in the coffin for Italy, and arguably one of the greatest goals ever scored, helping to create Brazil's glorious 4–1 win.

CARLOS ALBERTO – **Brazil** vs Italy

Brazil captain Carlos Alberto celebrates his team's fourth goal against Italy's goalkeeper Enrico Albertosi. Final score: Brazil 4 Italy 1, 21 June 1970.

1. Take on **Juliano**
2. Tackle **Brito**
3. Ball recovery **Tostão**
4. Pass **Tostão**
5. Pass **Piazza**
6. Pass **Clodoaldo**
7. Pass **Pelé**
8. Pass **Gérson**
9. Take on **Clodoaldo**
10. Good skill **Clodoaldo**
11. Challenge **Rivera**
12. Challenge **De Sisti**
13. Pass **Clodoaldo**
14. Pass **Rivelino**
15. Pass **Jairzinho**
16. Pass **Pelé**
17. Goal **Alberto**

KEY

Ball movement ⎯⎯⎯	Player with ball ··············
Shot ⎯⎯⎯⚽	Player without ball ············

ANATOLIY BYSHOVETS – USSR vs Belgium

1. Lay-off **Van Himst**
2. Ball recovery **Muntyan**
3. Pass **Muntyan**
4. Pass **Khmelnytskyi**
5. Goal **Byshovets**

CLODOALDO – Brazil vs Uruguay

1. Ball recovery **Alberto**
2. Pass **Alberto**
3. Pass **Gérson**
4. Pass **Piazza**
5. Pass **Rivelino**
6. Pass **Everaldo**
7. Pass **Clodoaldo**
8. Through ball **Tostão**
9. Goal **Clodoaldo**

JAIRZINHO – Brazil vs Uruguay

1. Pass **Espárrago**
2. Interception **Piazza**
3. Pass **Fontes**
4. Ball recovery **Jairzinho**
5. Pass **Jairzinho**
6. Flick-on **Pelé**
7. Pass **Tostão**
8. Take on **Jairzinho**
9. Challenge **Matosas**
10. Goal **Jairzinho**

PELÉ – Brazil vs Czechoslovakia

1. Pass **Adamec**
2. Interception **Everaldo**
3. Ball recovery **Everaldo**
4. Pass **Everaldo**
5. Pass **Rivelino**
6. Turnover **Gérson**
7. Pass **Brito**
8. Pass **Alberto**
9. Pass **Rivelino**
10. Pass (chipped) **Gérson**
11. Goal **Pelé**

THE PERFECT WORLD CUP PENALTY

To place or to blast? That is the question facing World Cup penalty-takers under the intense pressure of the glaring floodlights, thousands of expectant fans and their teammates unable to look away. In a World Cup tie the hopes of a nation lie on the quality of the execution. Some, like Andreas Brehme in 1990, have the steady composure to help their sides lift the Jules Rimet, whereas others, such as England's Chris Waddle's high-and-wide miss in 1990, led only to the shattering of millions of hearts. So where would you aim *your* penalty kick?

TOP LEFT

96% SCORED

49 GOALS SCORED
2 PENALTIES SAVED

HIGH CENTRE

94% SCORED

BOTTOM LEFT

80% SCORED

104 GOALS SCORED
26 PENALTIES SAVED

LOW CENTRE

69% SCORED

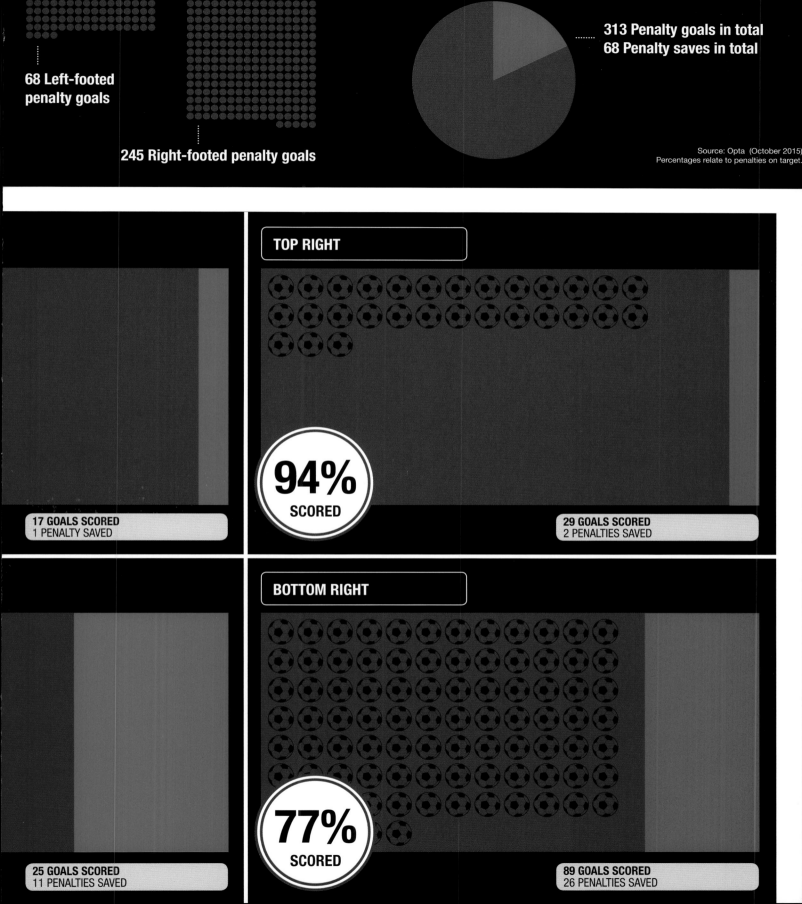

68 Left-footed penalty goals

245 Right-footed penalty goals

313 Penalty goals in total
68 Penalty saves in total

Source: Opta (October 2015)
Percentages relate to penalties on target.

TOP RIGHT

94%
SCORED

17 GOALS SCORED
1 PENALTY SAVED

29 GOALS SCORED
2 PENALTIES SAVED

BOTTOM RIGHT

77%
SCORED

25 GOALS SCORED
11 PENALTIES SAVED

89 GOALS SCORED
26 PENALTIES SAVED

EVOLUTION OF FORMATIONS

1872–1967

Every team has ten outfield players. What has proved critical over the years is not just how those players perform, but where. Formation is a key tactical element and, as these diagrams show, it is continually evolving. We can see the attack-heavy teams that dominated the early years of the game gradually becoming more balanced, with stronger midfields and defence.

1872

1-2-7 Formation

England

1889

The Pyramid (2-3-5)

Preston North End

1930

The WM Formation

Arsenal

" [Going behind] didn't bother us at all... We just knew we could turn the game around. "

Djalma Santos, Brazil's
1958 FIFA World Cup defender

Brazil's employment of a 4-2-4 formation helped them to victory in the 1958 FIFA World Cup.

1934

Danubian School

Austria

1938

The Metodo Formation

Italy

1953

The Diagonal Formation

Hungary

1958

4-2-4 Formation

Brazil

1961

3-3-4 Formation

Tottenham Hotspur

1967

Catenaccio

Internazionale Milano

EVOLUTION OF FORMATIONS

1971–2017

1971

4-3-3 Formation

Ajax

1990

Wing-backs Formation

Germany

1998

4-4-2 Formation

Manchester United

2003

2006

2012

e "False 9" F

Spain

From the 1970s onwards, the 4-4-2 formation became synonymous with the modern game. Here was a system that focused on passing and tackling in the central zones of the pitch and enabled increasingly fit midfielders to bolster both attacks and defences. It seemed the evolution had reached its conclusion. However, the search for any slight advantage meant coaches kept on tinkering. "Wingless wonder" teams and fluid "total football" line-ups were followed by wing-backs, "false 9s", pyramids and Christmas trees. Brazilian coach Carlos Alberto Parreira once predicted 4-6-0 as the "formation of the future" – and some might claim we are edging ever closer to that prophesy.

The pace and attacking skills of Tottenham Hotspur and England's Kyle Walker (on left) were integral to the success of the club's wing-back formation in 2017.

2014

4-5-1 Formation

Chelsea

2017

3-4-1-2 Formation

Tottenham Hotspur

" When you have full-backs like ours, Danny Rose or Kyle Walker, they can play forward as offensive players. We tried to put them in a better position to try and play more like wing-backs. That was our idea, and then to play with two strikers. "

Mauricio Pochettino, manager Tottenham Hotspur

LA LIGA TITLE WINNERS

La Liga, the elite league of Spanish football, was born in 1929 from a core group of teams playing for the national knockout competition, the Copa del Rey. Sixty different teams have since competed in the league and nine different teams have lifted the trophy. The league has been dominated by Barcelona and Real Madrid, the giants of Spanish football, while Athletic Bilbao, Atlético Madrid and Valencia deserve honourable mentions too. With its teams faring well in European competition, La Liga is currently rated the best league in Europe.

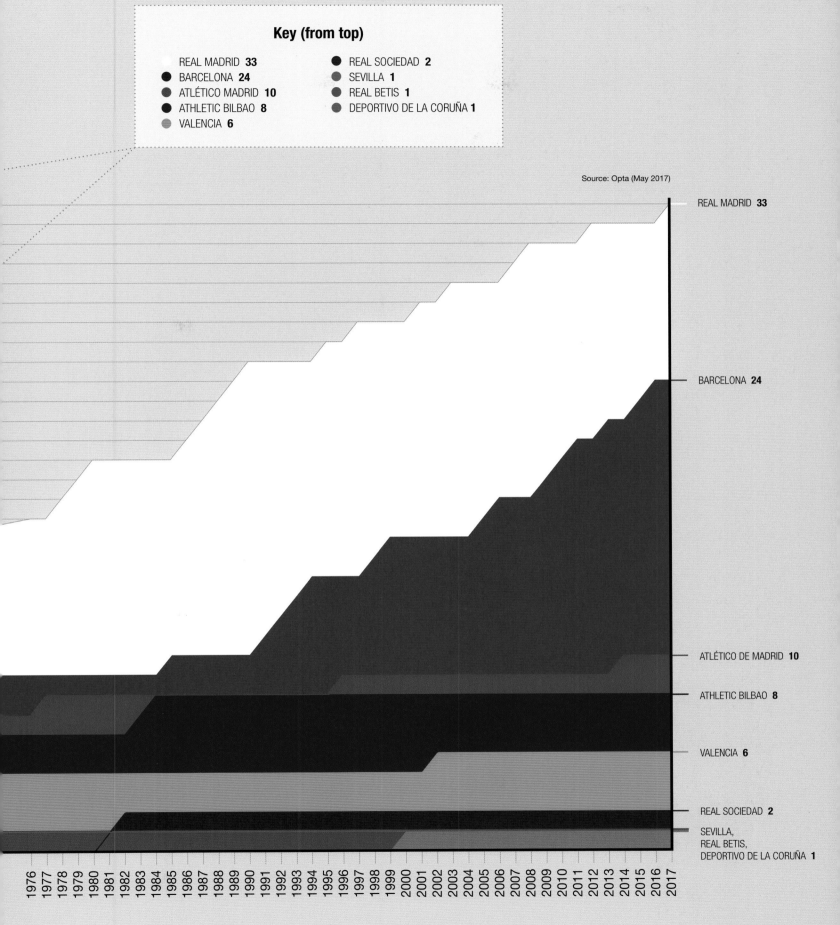

Key (from top)

- REAL MADRID **33**
- BARCELONA **24**
- ATLÉTICO MADRID **10**
- ATHLETIC BILBAO **8**
- VALENCIA **6**
- REAL SOCIEDAD **2**
- SEVILLA **1**
- REAL BETIS **1**
- DEPORTIVO DE LA CORUÑA **1**

Source: Opta (May 2017)

REAL MADRID **33**

BARCELONA **24**

ATLÉTICO DE MADRID **10**

ATHLETIC BILBAO **8**

VALENCIA **6**

REAL SOCIEDAD **2**

SEVILLA,
REAL BETIS,
DEPORTIVO DE LA CORUÑA **1**

1976 1977 1978 1979 1980 1981 1982 1983 1984 1985 1986 1987 1988 1989 1990 1991 1992 1993 1994 1995 1996 1997 1998 1999 2000 2001 2002 2003 2004 2005 2006 2007 2008 2009 2010 2011 2012 2013 2014 2015 2016 2017

SCOTTISH LEAGUE TITLE WINNERS

The Scottish Football League was established in 1890 just two years after its English counterpart. Dumbarton captured the first two titles, but the domination of Glasgow's Old Firm – Celtic and Rangers – soon took hold. The top flight was reorganized into the Scottish Premier League (1998–2013) and the Scottish Premiership (since 2013) – comprising 12 clubs since the 2000–01 season. All clubs play each other three times before the league is split in half, with teams playing a further single match against each of their section.

NO CHAMPIONSHIP FROM 1939-1946

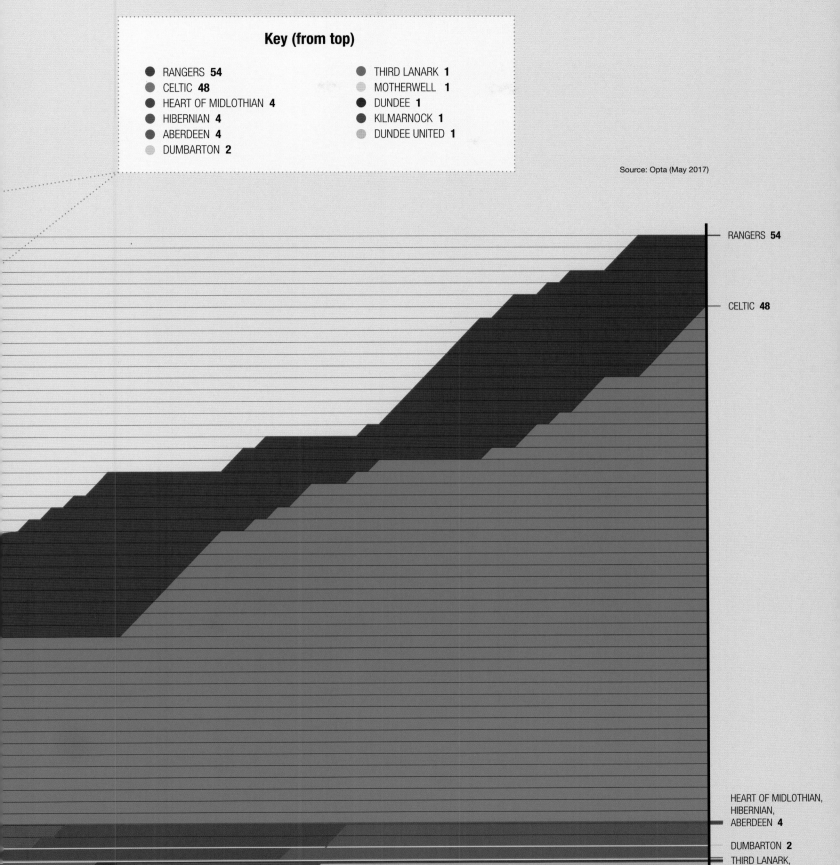

Key (from top)

- RANGERS **54**
- CELTIC **48**
- HEART OF MIDLOTHIAN **4**
- HIBERNIAN **4**
- ABERDEEN **4**
- DUMBARTON **2**
- THIRD LANARK **1**
- MOTHERWELL **1**
- DUNDEE **1**
- KILMARNOCK **1**
- DUNDEE UNITED **1**

Source: Opta (May 2017)

RANGERS **54**

CELTIC **48**

HEART OF MIDLOTHIAN, HIBERNIAN, ABERDEEN **4**

DUMBARTON **2**

THIRD LANARK, MOTHERWELL, DUNDEE, KILMARNOCK, DUNDEE UNITED **1**

1956 1957 1958 1959 1960 1961 1962 1963 1964 1965 1966 1967 1968 1969 1970 1971 1972 1973 1974 1975 1976 1977 1978 1979 1980 1981 1982 1983 1984 1985 1986 1987 1988 1989 1990 1991 1992 1993 1994 1995 1996 1997 1998 1999 2000 2001 2002 2003 2004 2005 2006 2007 2008 2009 2010 2011 2012 2013 2014 2015 2016 2017

SERIE A TITLE WINNERS

Serie A has been the top-flight tournament in Italian soccer since the 1929–30 season. Rated as one of the most entertaining and thrilling leagues in the world, Serie A has a reputation for highly tactical performances and players with virtuoso and prodigious technical ability. However, the league has also been rocked by controversy and scandal, including the 2006 *Calciopoli*, as it became known, where some top teams were accused of rigging games by selecting biased referees. The winner of the league is awarded the *Scudetto*, a badge with the colours of the Italian flag, to be worn on the champions' shirts the following season.

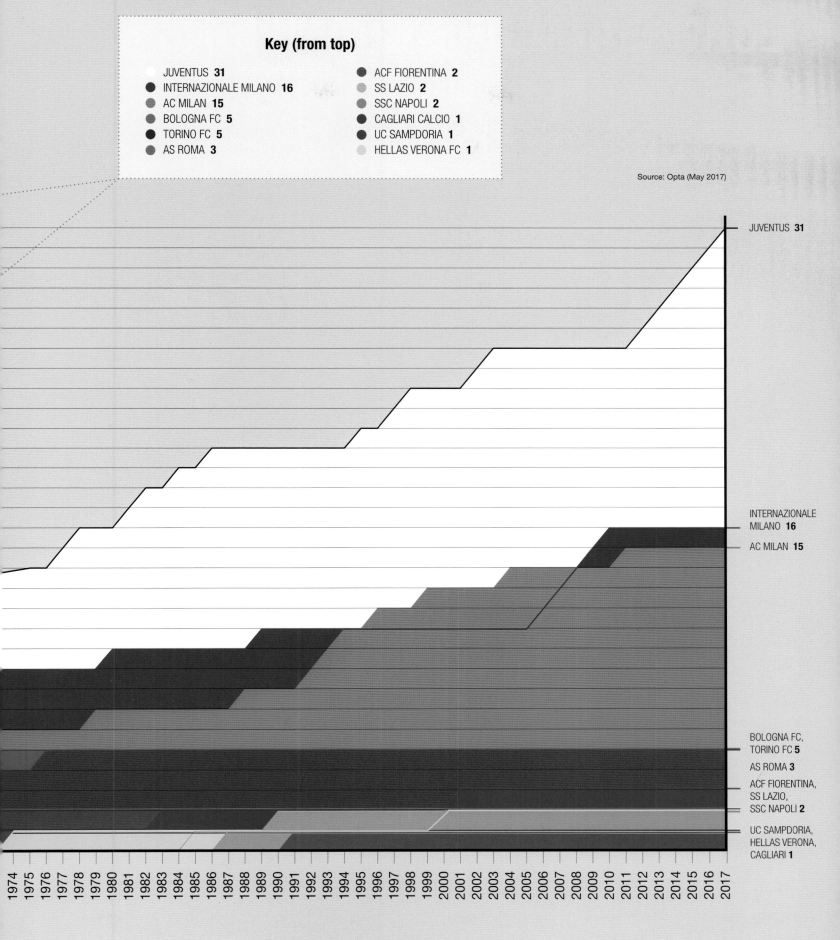

Key (from top)

- ○ JUVENTUS **31**
- ● INTERNAZIONALE MILANO **16**
- ◍ AC MILAN **15**
- ● BOLOGNA FC **5**
- ● TORINO FC **5**
- ● AS ROMA **3**
- ● ACF FIORENTINA **2**
- ◔ SS LAZIO **2**
- ◍ SSC NAPOLI **2**
- ● CAGLIARI CALCIO **1**
- ● UC SAMPDORIA **1**
- ◌ HELLAS VERONA FC **1**

Source: Opta (May 2017)

JUVENTUS **31**

INTERNAZIONALE MILANO **16**

AC MILAN **15**

BOLOGNA FC, TORINO FC **5**

AS ROMA **3**

ACF FIORENTINA, SS LAZIO, SSC NAPOLI **2**

UC SAMPDORIA, HELLAS VERONA, CAGLIARI **1**

1974 1975 1976 1977 1978 1979 1980 1981 1982 1983 1984 1985 1986 1987 1988 1989 1990 1991 1992 1993 1994 1995 1996 1997 1998 1999 2000 2001 2002 2003 2004 2005 2006 2007 2008 2009 2010 2011 2012 2013 2014 2015 2016 2017

EUROPEAN CUP & CHAMPIONS LEAGUE RECORD GOALSCORERS

Real Madrid strikers have dominated the table of goalscorers in the Champions League and its forerunner, the European Cup. Legendary striker Alfredo di Stéfano led the table for many years before he was succeeded by Raúl in 2007. Barcelona's Lionel Messi managed to take the record in November 2014, only to be equalled by Cristiano Ronaldo a day later. The great rivals continue to spar for the crown, the Real striker scoring an astonishing nine goals in the 2017 knockout stages and notching his hundredth goal with a quarter-final hat-trick against Bayern.

15 Manchester United
90 Real Madrid

1. Cristiano Ronaldo

105 Total goals scored

94 Barcelona

2. Lionel Messi

94 Total goals scored

5 Schalke
66 Real Madrid

3. Raúl

71 Total goals scored

13 Real Madrid   8 PSV
35 Manchester United

4. Ruud van Nistelrooy

56 Total goals scored

12 Lyon
39 Real Madrid

5. Karim Benzema

51 Total goals scored

8 Barcelona   7 Monaco
35 Arsenal

6. Thierry Henry

50 Total goals scored

49 Real Madrid

7. Alfredo Di Stéfano

49 Total goals scored

15 Dynamo Kiev   4 Chelsea
29 AC Milan

8. Andriy Shevchenko

48 Total goals scored

9 AC Milan   6 Inter
20 Paris Saint-Germain
6 Ajax
4 Barcelona
3 Juventus

9. Zlatan Ibrahimović

48 Total goals scored

"...I want to consistently play well and win titles...
I'm only at the beginning."

ristiano Ronaldo

46 Benfica

0. Eusébio

46 Total goals scored

17 Juventus

29 AC Milan

1. Filippo Inzaghi

46 Total goals scored

5 Marseille   3 Galatasaray

36 Chelsea

2. Didier Drogba

44 Total goals scored

Source: Opta (June 2017)

EUROPEAN CUP & CHAMPIONS LEAGUE RECORD GOALSCORERS

42 Juventus

13. Alessandro Del Piero

42 Total goals scored

17 Borussia Dortmund

23 Bayern München

14. Robert Lewandowski

40 Total goals scored

39 Bayern München

15. Thomas Müller

39 Total goals scored

1 Honvéd

35 Real Madrid

16. Ferenc Puskás

36 Total goals scored

34 Bayern München

17. Gerd Müller

34 Total goals scored

9 Monaco · Va

17 Real Madrid

Liv

18. Fernando Morientes

33 Total goals scored

5 Real Madrid

25 AC Milan

19. Kaká

30 Total Goals Scored

30 Real Madrid

20. Paco Gento

30 Total Goals Scored

30 Manchester United

21. Wayne Rooney

30 Total Goals Scored

10 Inter   3 Chelsea

16 Barcelona

1 Mallorca

22. Samuel Eto'o

30 Total goals scored

3 PSV   2 Chelsea

23 Bayern München

1 Real Madrid

23. Arjen Robben

29 Total goals scored

4 Monaco

25 Juventus

24. David Trezeguet

29 Total goals scored

25. Roy Makaay

12 Deportivo de La Coruña
17 Bayern München

29 Total goals scored

26. Patrick Kluivert

9 Ajax
20 Barcelona

29 Total goals scored

27. Ryan Giggs

28 Manchester United

28 Total goals scored

28. Jean-Pierre Papin

7 Milan
2 Bayern München
19 Marseille

28 Total goals scored

29. Rivaldo

3 Olympiacos
2 AC Milan
22 Barcelona

27 Total goals scored

30. Sergio Agüero

5 Atlético de Madrid
22 Manchester City

27 Total goals scored

"If he kicked the ball once, he scored two goals."

Zoltán Czibor on his International teammate Ferenc Puskás, scorer of a first-half hat-trick for Real Madrid in the 1962 UEFA European Cup Final

Source: Opta (June 2017)

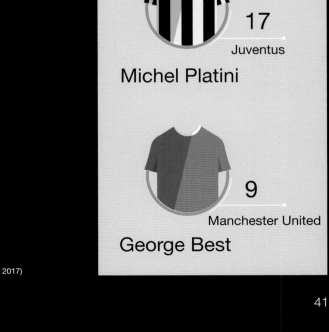

Legendary Players

21 Liverpool
Steven Gerrard

18 Ajax
Johan Cruyff

17 Roma
Francesco Totti

17 Juventus
Michel Platini

9 Manchester United
George Best

PREMIER LEAGUE TITLE WINNERS

The Premier League was formed in 1992. It is far and away the wealthiest league, most of the clubs featuring among the top 50 richest football brands in the world. Since its formation, the Premier League has been contested by 47 clubs, and games are broadcast in more than 200 countries. For many years the title was fought over by the "big four" – Manchester United, Arsenal, Chelsea and Liverpool – but Manchester City and more recently Tottenham Hotspur have joined them. Even more surprising, then, was Leicester City's triumph against all odds in 2016.

Note: For the first three seasons of its existence, the Premier League comprised 22 teams rather than 20, as became the norm.

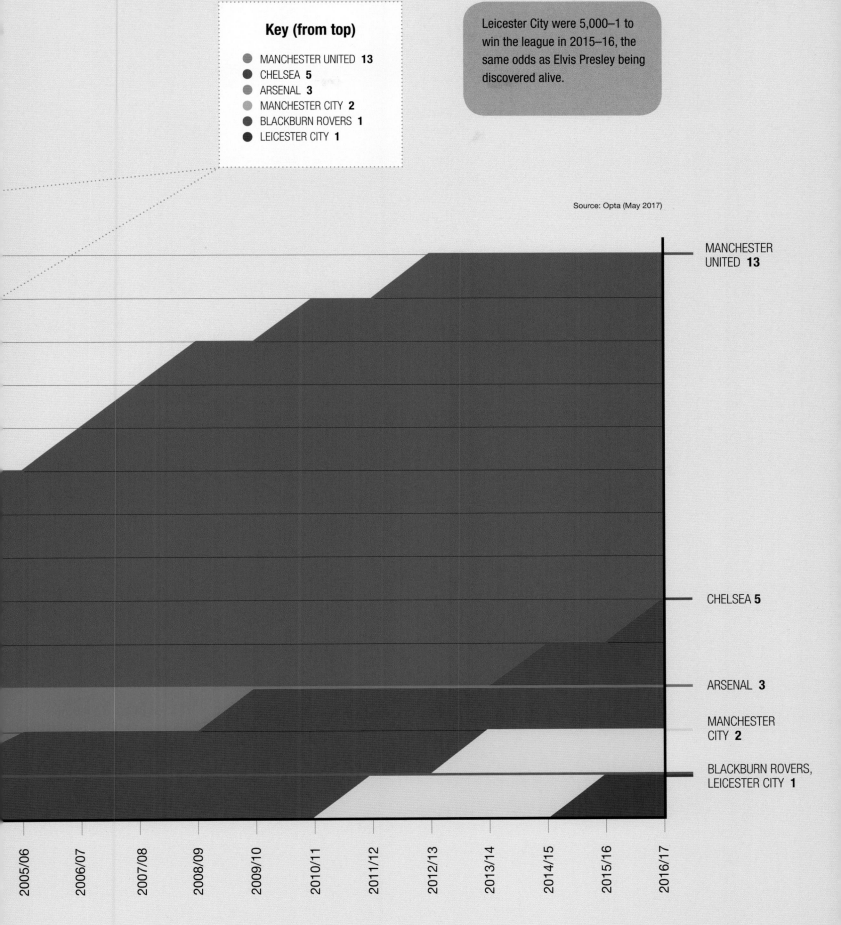

Key (from top)

- MANCHESTER UNITED **13**
- CHELSEA **5**
- ARSENAL **3**
- MANCHESTER CITY **2**
- BLACKBURN ROVERS **1**
- LEICESTER CITY **1**

Leicester City were 5,000–1 to win the league in 2015–16, the same odds as Elvis Presley being discovered alive.

Source: Opta (May 2017)

MANCHESTER UNITED **13**

CHELSEA **5**

ARSENAL **3**

MANCHESTER CITY **2**

BLACKBURN ROVERS, LEICESTER CITY **1**

2005/06 · 2006/07 · 2007/08 · 2008/09 · 2009/10 · 2010/11 · 2011/12 · 2012/13 · 2013/14 · 2014/15 · 2015/16 · 2016/17

1974 WORLD CUP GOALS

In 1974 West Germany hosted (and won) a memorable World Cup that first gave us the Cruyff Turn, Zaire becoming the first African team to qualify, a Cold War classic between East and West Germany and the "total football" displayed by the Netherlands. Goals came in all shapes and sizes, but we all remember the two belters from West Germany's Paul Breitner, Peter Lorimer's volley for Scotland against Zaire, Haiti's Emmanuel Sanon outpacing the Italian defence and Johan Cruyff's stunner against Brazil – a goal that crowned the Dutchman Player of the Tournament.

JOHAN CRUYFF – Netherlands vs Brazil

Fifty-two thousand fans watched Johan Cruyff score his second goal for the Netherlands against Brazil, 3 July 1974.

1. Free kick taken **Haan**
2. Pass **van Hanegem**
3. Pass (chipped) **Rijsbergen**
4. Pass **Krol**
5. Pass **Rensenbrink**
6. Pass (cross, chipped, long ball) **Krol**
7. Goal **Cruyff**

KEY

Ball movement	————	Player with ball · · · · · · · · ·
Shot	————⚽	Player without ball · · · · · · · · ·

PAUL BREITNER – West Germany vs Chile

1. Take on **Rodríguez**
2. Tackle **Hoeneß**
3. Ball recovery **Hoeneß**
4. Pass **Hoeneß**
5. Pass **Overath**
6. Pass **Müller**
7. Pass **Hoeneß**
8. Pass **Breitner**
9. Pass **Hoeneß**
10. Pass **Overath**
11. Pass **Heynckes**
12. Pass **Hoeneß**
13. Pass **Beckenbauer**
14. Goal **Breitner**

JOHAN CRUYFF – Netherlands vs Argentina

1. Pass **Telch**
2. Interception **Neeskens**
3. Pass **Neeskens**
4. Pass (chipped) **Rep**
5. Pass **Haan**
6. Lay-off **Rensenbrink**
7. Pass **Krol**
8. Pass **van Hanegem**
9. Pass **Jansen**
10. Attempt saved **van Hanegem**
11. Save (parried danger) **Carnevali**
12. Goal **Cruyff**

RIVELINO – Brazil vs Zaire

1. Pass **Jairzinho**
2. Pass (chipped) **Carpegiani**
3. Pass **Edu**
4. Pass **Marinho**
5. Pass **Jairzinho**
6. Goal **Rivelino**

JÜRGEN SPARWASSER – East Germany vs West Germany

1. Head pass **Flohe**
2. Keeper pick-up **Croy**
3. Keeper throw **Croy**
4. Pass (long ball, chipped) **Hamann**
5. Take on **Sparwasser**
6. Challenge **Höttges**
7. Goal **Sparwasser**

BUNDESLIGA TITLE WINNERS

The Bundesliga was formed in 1963 to bring professionalism to the German game. The early years saw five different champions in five seasons before two promoted teams, Bayern München and Borussia Mönchengladbach, went on to dominate the league, both winning three successive titles. Bayern would continue to lead even after the league was revolutionized after 1989 at the unification of Germany. Various clubs – the latest being Borussia Dortmund – have risen to challenge Bayern's supremacy, but "FC Hollywood", as other teams' fans have continued to call them, remain the undisputed giants of the Bundesliga.

Key (clockwise from top)

- BAYERN MÜNCHEN **26**
- BORUSSIA DORTMUND **5**
- BORUSSIA MÖNCHENGLADBACH **5**
- SV WERDER BREMEN **4**
- HAMBURGER SV **3**
- VFB STUTTGART **3**

- 1. FC KAISERSLAUTERN **2**
- 1. FC KÖLN **2**
- EINTRACHT BRAUNSCHWEIG **1**
- TSV 1860 MÜNCHEN **1**
- 1. FC NÜRNBERG **1**
- VFL WOLFSBURG **1**

Source: Opta (May 2017)

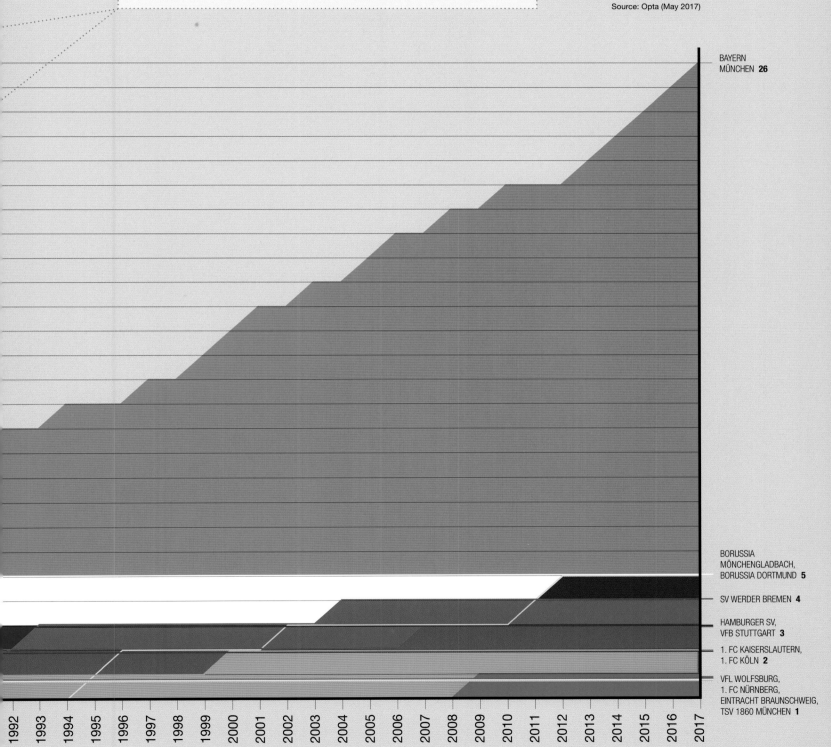

BAYERN MÜNCHEN **26**

BORUSSIA MÖNCHENGLADBACH, BORUSSIA DORTMUND **5**

SV WERDER BREMEN **4**

HAMBURGER SV, VFB STUTTGART **3**

1. FC KAISERSLAUTERN, 1. FC KÖLN **2**

VFL WOLFSBURG, 1. FC NÜRNBERG, EINTRACHT BRAUNSCHWEIG, TSV 1860 MÜNCHEN **1**

1992 1993 1994 1995 1996 1997 1998 1999 2000 2001 2002 2003 2004 2005 2006 2007 2008 2009 2010 2011 2012 2013 2014 2015 2016 2017

*Chile celebrate winning their second successive Copa
América championship after beating Argentina on penalties
at the MetLife Stadium in East Rutherford, USA.*

49

LONG-RANGE WORLD CUP GOALS

Everyone loves a shot at goal from far out, especially if it's on target and struck with an awesome power to match. In particular, long-range goals during World Cups are even more wondrous to behold because they instantly take on legendary status. Those long-rangers that live forever in the memory include Bobby Charlton's 25-yard strike against Mexico which fired up England's 1966 campaign, Arie Haan's 40-yard lightning-bolt as the Netherlands defeated Italy in 1978 and James Rodríguez's sensational chest and volley against Uruguay in 2014. All excellent goals, but where do they map in the long-range pantheon?

ARIE HAAN

Netherlands
vs
Italy

🎯 **36.71m**

🕐 **75:18**

ROUND 2
21-06-1978

PAUL BREITNER

West Germany
vs
Chile

🎯 **39.69m**

🕐 **15:50**

GROUP STAGE
14-06-1974

LOTHAR MATTHÄUS
West Germany
vs
Yugoslavia

 31.93m

 62:51

GROUP STAGE
10-06-1990

Source: Opta (October 2015)

ARIE HAAN
Netherlands
vs
West Germany

 31.41m

26:40

ROUND 2
18-06-1978

JOE COLE
England
vs
Sweden

 33.2m

33:04

GROUP STAGE
20-06-2006

RONALDINHO
Brazil
vs
England

 40.08m

49:02

QUARTER-FINAL
21-06-2002

NELINHO
Brazil
vs
Italy

31.86m

63:35

3RD PLACE MATCH
24-06-1978

51

WOMEN'S WORLD CUP TROPHIES AND GOALS

The first official Women's World Cup took place in China in 1991. There were 12 teams but no winners' prize money and no sponsor, while the matches lasted just 80 minutes. Since then, the women's game and the competition have grown beyond recognition with eight four-yearly tournaments. In Canada, in 2015, the qualifying rounds saw 134 nations compete for 24 places; 26.7 million TV viewers made the final the most-watched soccer game in American history and the victorious US team won $2 million in prize money.

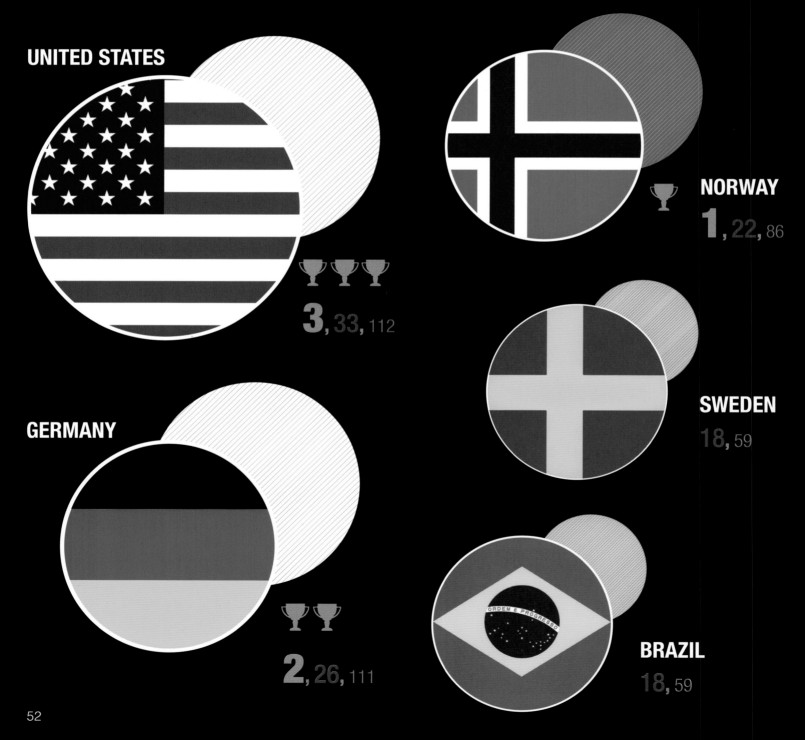

UNITED STATES

3, 33, 112

GERMANY

2, 26, 111

NORWAY

1, 22, 86

SWEDEN

18, 59

BRAZIL

18, 59

Source: Opta (October 2015)

PR CHINA
15, 52

FRANCE
6, 22

CAMEROON
2, 9

SWITZERLAND
1, 11

AUSTRALIA
5, 29

GHANA
1, 6

JAPAN
1, 13, 36

RUSSIA
4, 16

KOREA REPUBLIC
1, 5

COLOMBIA
1, 4

ENGLAND
10, 30

DENMARK
3, 19

THAILAND
1, 3

NIGERIA
3, 18

NETHERLANDS
1, 3

CHINESE TAIPEI
1, 2

CANADA
6, 30

DPR KOREA
3, 12

ITALY
3, 11

1 **TOURNAMENTS WON**
1 MATCHES WON
1 GOALS SCORED

53

1978 WORLD CUP GOALS

The "Tickertape Tournament" in 1978 was a bittersweet affair. It was set against an unsavoury political background, boycotted by Johan Cruyff (rated as the world's best player at the time) and disgraced by Scotland's Willie Johnston, who was sent home after a positive drug test. However, the tournament also gave us some unforgettable goals, including a magical finish by Scotland's Archie Gemmill, screamers from the Netherland's Arie Haan and Brazil's Nelinho, and a much-needed morale-boosting triumph for the host nation, Argentina, when they defeated the Netherlands 3–1, thanks to the tournament's top scorer, Mario Kempes, and his second goal of the day.

ARIE HAAN – **Netherlands** vs West Germany

Arie Haan's goal against West Germany (18 June 1978) helped the Dutch national team reach the 1978 World Cup final, where they were beaten by Argentina 3–1 in extra time.

1. Goal kick (long ball) **Maier**
2. Head pass **Brandts**
3. Ball recovery **Haan**
4. Pass **Haan**
5. Pass **Willy van de Kerkhof**
6. Pass **René van de Kerkhof**
7. Goal **Haan**

KEY

Ball movement	——	Player with ball	••••••••••••
Shot	——⚽	Player without ball	••••••••••••

ARCHIE GEMMILL – Scotland vs Netherlands

1. Free kick taken **Rioch**
2. Pass **Kennedy**
3. Take on **Dalglish**
4. Take on **Gemmill**
5. Tackle **Krol**
6. Good skill **Gemmill**
7. Challenge **Krol**
8. Take on **Gemmill**
9. Goal **Gemmill**

LEOPOLDO LUQUE – Argentina vs France

1. Goal kick **Fillol**
2. Pass **Olguín**
3. Pass **Ardiles**
4. Pass **Gallego**
5. Pass **Kempes**
6. Pass **Ardiles**
7. Goal **Luque**

NELINHO – Brazil vs Italy

1. Goal kick (long ball) **Zoff**
2. Interception **Cerezo**
3. Ball recovery **Mendonça**
4. Pass **Mendonça**
5. Pass **Cerezo**
6. Pass **Dinamite**
7. Goal **Nelinho**

KARL-HEINZ RUMMENIGGE – West Germany vs Mexico

1. Clearance **Rummenigge**
2. Lay-off **Fischer**
3. Pass (chipped) **Dieter Müller**
4. Pass **Flohe**
5. Pass (cross, chipped, long ball) **Fischer**
6. Good skill **Hansi Müller**
7. Lay-off **Hansi Müller**
8. Goal **Rummenigge**

PREMIER LEAGUE EVER-PRESENTS

The relegation of Aston Villa to the Championship in 2016 reduced the survivors from the founding season of the Premier League to six. Of the 47 teams that have played in the top league, all but these six have spent time in lower leagues – Coventry City, Swindon Town, Blackpool, Portsmouth and Bradford City have all subsequently fallen as far as the fourth tier. Brighton & Hove Albion and Huddersfield Town's 2017 promotion to the top flight will make them the 48th and 49th clubs to play in the Premier League.

Source: Opta (May 2017)

LEAGUE POSITION AT END OF SEASON

YEAR (END OF SEASON)

KEY:

MAY
JUNE
JULY
AUGUST
SEPTEMBER
OCTOBER
NOVEMBER
DECEMBER
JANUARY
FEBRUARY
MARCH
APRIL
MAY

━━━ ARSENAL
━━━ CHELSEA
━━━ EVERTON
━━━ LIVERPOOL
━━━ MANCHESTER UNITED
━━━ TOTTENHAM

① CHANGE OF MANAGER

━━━ PARTICIPATED IN CHAMPIONS LEAGUE

🏆 PREMIER LEAGUE TITLE WIN

🏆 CHAMPIONS LEAGUE TITLE WIN

Source: Opta May 2017

Note: For the first three seasons of its existence, the Premier League comprised 22 teams rather than 20, as became the established contingent.

Avram Grant 9/20/07
Felipe Scolari 7/1/08
David Moyes 7/1/13
José Mourinho 6/3/13
André Villas-Boas 6/22/11
André Villas-Boas 7/3/12
José Mourinho 5/27/16
10 Guus Hiddink 2/16/09
11 Carlo Ancelotti 7/1/09
16
Rafael Benitez 11/21/12
18 Tim Sherwood 12/16/13
19 Mauricio Pochettino 5/27/14
Roberto Di Matteo 3/4/12
17 Eddie Newton / Steve Holland 12/18/15
18 Guus Hiddink 12/20/15
Roberto Martinez 6/5/13
3 Ryan Giggs 4/22/14
4 Louis van Gaal 7/14/14
14 Clive Allen/ Alex Inglethorpe 2/16/09
15 Juande Ramos 10/29/07
Roy Hodgson 7/1/10
Kenny Dalglish 1/8/11
Jürgen Klopp 10/8/15
Antonio Conte 7/1/16
Brendan Rodgers 6/1/12
Harry Redknapp 10/25/08
10 David Unsworth / Joe Royle 5/12/16
11 Ronald Koeman 6/14/16

MAY 2006   MAY 2007   MAY 2008   MAY 2009   MAY 2010   MAY 2011   MAY 2012   MAY 2013   MAY 2014   MAY 2015   MAY 2016   MAY 2017

1 2 3 4 5 6 7 8 9 10 11 12 13 14 15 16 17 18 19 20

1982 WORLD CUP GOALS

Spain's 1982 World Cup finals saw 24 teams play in a format involving two group stages.
It was never used again. The tournament became the battleground for two of the greatest matches ever
played in World Cup history. Italy's Paolo Rossi hit a hat-trick in an amazing 3–2 defeat of Brazil and, after a
3–3 draw, West Germany overcame France in the first ever World Cup penalty shoot-out. Memorable goals
included an overhead bicycle kick by Germany's Klaus Fischer, a sublime chip from Brazil's Éder and a
strike from his compatriot, Sócrates, which proved completely unstoppable. However, it was Tardelli's goal
(and his celebration) against West Germany in the final that we all remember the most.

MARCO TARDELLI – Italy vs West Germany

Italy's Marco Tardelli celebrates scoring his goal against West Germany during the 1982 World Cup final. Italy won the match 3–1, 11 July 1982.

1. Pass **Conti**
2. Pass **Rossi**
3. Pass **Scirea**
4. Pass **Bergomi**
5. Pass **Scirea**
6. Goal **Tardelli**

KEY

Ball movement	——	Player with ball ··············
Shot	——⚽	Player without ball ··············

ZBIGNIEW BONIEK – Poland vs Belgium

1. Goal kick **Młynarczyk**
2. Pass **Janas**
3. Pass **Żmuda**
4. Pass **Buncol**
5. Pass **Majewski**
6. Pass (long ball) **Buncol**
7. Pass **Janas**
8. Pass (chipped, long ball) **Buncol**
9. Pass **Dziuba**
10. Take on **Lato**
11. Challenge **Millecamps**
12. Pull-back **Lato**
13. Goal **Boniek**

BRUNO CONTI – Italy vs Peru

1. Goal kick **Zoff**
2. Pass **Scirea**
3. Pass **Conti**
4. Pass (long ball, chipped) **Tardelli**
5. Pass **Cabrini**
6. Pass **Antognoni**
7. Challenge **Velásquez**
8. Good skill **Conti**
9. Take on **Conti**
10. Goal **Conti**

KLAUS FISCHER – West Germany vs France

1. Corner taken **Kaltz**
2. Clearance **Platini**
3. Pass **Breitner**
4. Pass (chipped, cross) **Kaltz**
5. Head pass **Kaltz**
6. Pass (long ball) **Rummenigge**
7. Pass **Förster**
8. Pass (chipped, cross, long ball) **Littbarski**
9. Head pass **Rummenigge**
10. Goal **Fischer**

SÓCRATES – Brazil vs Italy

1. Throw in **Leandro**
2. Pass **Oscar**
3. Pass **Sócrates**
4. Good skill **Zico**
5. Take on **Zico**
6. Challenge **Gentile**
7. Through ball **Zico**
8. Goal **Sócrates**

WORLD CUP GOALS BY BODY PART

"They all count!" It may be an old footballing cliché but it is as true in World Cup finals as it is anywhere else. For every exquisite shot curled in from the edge of the penalty area, there is a ricochet off the shin from two yards. For every perfectly timed scissor-kick, there is a vicious and ugly toe-punt just to make sure the ball goes in. When it comes down to the wire in a World Cup match, any goal will do.

886

RIGHT-FOOT GOALS

Source: Opta (October 2015)

486

LEFT-FOOT GOALS

300 HEADED GOALS

30 OWN GOALS

Of the 1712 goals scored in the World Cup only 30 have been own goals – less than two per cent. Perhaps the strangest own goal ever scored, so far, belongs to Greece's Vasilis Torosidis during the World Cup qualifying game against Romania in 2014, whose intended left-foot clearance from inside the penalty box ended up being fished out from the back of his own net.

10 OTHER GOALS

The most notorious scoring body part belongs to Maradona's "Hand of God" against England in 1986. Also worthy of a mention are Clint Dempsey's "Groin Goal" for the USA against Portugal in 2014 and the great Jairzinho "chesting" the ball in to score Brazil's second goal in the 1970 final.

SERIE A GOALS

Goals are said to be hard to come by in an often defensively minded Serie A, but if you are good enough… It certainly wasn't a problem for 1930s star Silvio Piola, whose record of 274 goals in 537 games – set with Novarro, Lazio, Juventus and others – looks unassailable. Even the great Francesco Totti had eventually to concede that the target was out of sight. Among the young guns in the league, only Inter's Mauro Icardi (82 goals), Torino's Andrea Belotti, (67) and Lazio's Keita (25) look capable of inclusion in future charts.

> "When Totti plays – but it's the same in training and even when he's playing with his boy – he's the Muhammad Ali of football, always looking to land that knockout blow: to swing the punch no one else can see."

Roma coach Luciano Spalletti

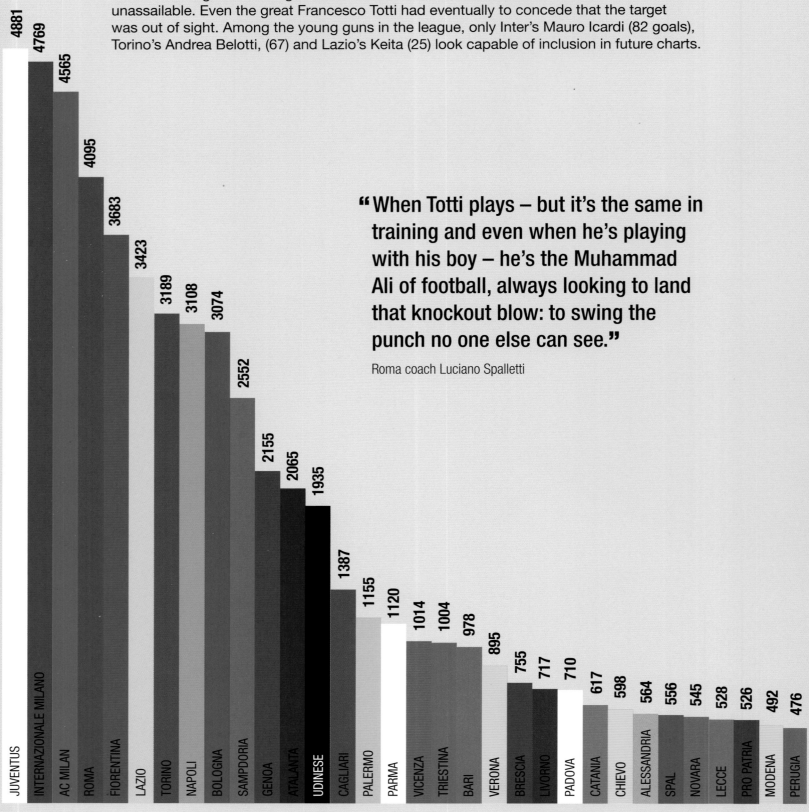

Team	Goals
JUVENTUS	4881
INTERNAZIONALE MILANO	4769
AC MILAN	4565
ROMA	4095
FIORENTINA	3683
LAZIO	3423
TORINO	3189
NAPOLI	3108
BOLOGNA	3074
SAMPDORIA	2552
GENOA	2155
ATALANTA	2065
UDINESE	1935
CAGLIARI	1387
PALERMO	1155
PARMA	1120
VICENZA	1014
TRIESTINA	1004
BARI	978
VERONA	895
BRESCIA	755
LIVORNO	717
PADOVA	710
CATANIA	617
CHIEVO	598
ALESSANDRIA	564
SPAL	556
NOVARA	545
LECCE	528
PRO PATRIA	526
MODENA	492
PERUGIA	476

FRANCESCO TOTTI	250	ANTONIO DI NATALE	209	ALBERTO GILARDINO	188	ALESSANDRO DEL PIERO	183
LUCA TONI	157	FILIPPO INZAGHI	156	GABRIEL BATISTUTA	155	HERNÁN CRESPO	153
MARCO DI VAIO	143	CHRISTIAN VIERI	141	VINCENZO MONTELLA	141	ENRICO CHIESA	137
GIUSEPPE SIGNORI	128	ANDRIY SHEVCHENKO	127	DAVID TREZEGUET	123	ZLATAN IBRAHIMOVIĆ	122
CRISTIANO LUCARELLI	120	ANTONIO CASSANO	113	EDINSON CAVANI	112	NICOLA AMORUSO	110
FABIO QUAGLIARELLA	108	GIAMPAOLO PAZZINI	107	SERGIO PELLISSIER	107	FABRIZIO MICCOLI	103
ADRIAN MUTU	103	TOMMASO ROCCHI	102	OLIVER BIERHOFF	100	ROBERTO BAGGIO	96
MIRKO VUČINIĆ	96	GONZALO HIGUAÍN	95	MARCO BORRIELLO	95	MAREK HAMŠÍK	93
VINCENZO IAQUINTA	89	ALESSANDRO MATRI	87	DIEGO MILITO	86	ROBERTO MUZZI	86
AMAURI	85						

Il Re di Roma (The King of Rome), Francesco Totti retired from his beloved club, Roma, at the end of the 2016–17 season. The five-time Italian footballer of the year, European Golden Boot holder (2007) and World Cup winner (2006) scored his first goal for the Giallorossi on the opening day of the 1994–95 season. His 250th and final league goal came in September 2016 at the age of 40. His loyalty to Roma has meant he has never achieved Champions League success, but there is no doubt of his status in the game. When Roma met Barcelona in a pre-season friendly, Lionel Messi uploaded a shot of him in Totti's shirt with the caption: "A great! What a phenomenon!!" It got 1.8 million likes.

Source: Opta (May 2017)
Player data: 1994–95 to 2016–17
Colour relates to the team for which the player scored the highest number of goals.

ASCOLI 425
VENEZIA 413
COMO 411
EMPOLI 404
CESENA 364
FOGGIA 360
SIENA 356
LUCCHESE 347
REGGINA 324
PIACENZA 281
AVELLINO 268
PRO VERCELLI 251
CREMONESE 222
PESCARA 205
SASSUOLO 199
MANTOVA 182
PISA 174
LIGURIA 168
MESSINA 165
VARESE 164
CATANZARO 156
CASALE 149
LEGNANO 111
SAMPIERDARENESE 93
LECCO 84
SALERNITANA 83
REGGIANA 81
ANCONA 60
CARPI 37
FROSINONE 35
CROTONE 34
TERNANA 33
TREVISO 24
PISTOIESE 19

GAMES TO REACH 100 GOALS

t's true that you need more than star power in order to score goals consistently. You need a little luck, talented teammates and a crumbling opposition too. But when it comes to scoring a century (and more) for their club, the Premier League players below have shown they've got what it takes to become truly magical and, as a result, have joined an elite squad of top-scoring centurions. For all strikers, this is the benchmark worth getting out of bed for.

Source: Opta (May 2017)

The players' colours below represents the team colour for which the player scored their 100th goal

ALAN SHEARER 124 Games

100th Goal: 30-12-95
Blackburn Rovers
vs Tottenham Hotspur
41st min

SERGIO AGÜERO 147 Games

100th Goal: 19-04-16
Manchester City
vs Newcastle United
14th min

THIERRY HENRY 160 Games

100th Goal: 10-02-04
Arsenal
vs Southampton
31st min

IAN WRIGHT 173 Games

100th Goal: 13-09-97
Arsenal
vs Bolton Wanderers
81st min

ROBBIE FOWLER 175 Games

100th Goal: 16-01-99
Liverpool
vs Southampton
37th min

LES FERDINAND 178 Games

100th Goal: 11-05-97
Newcastle United
vs Nottingham Forest
23rd min

MICHAEL OWEN 185 Games

100th Goal: 26-04-03
Liverpool vs
West Bromwich Albion
49th min

ANDREW COLE 185 Games

100th Goal: 17-02-99
Manchester United
vs Arsenal
60th min

ROBIN VAN PERSIE 197 Games

100th Goal: 02-09-12
Manchester United
vs Southampton
90th min

JIMMY FLOYD HASSELBAINK 200 Games

100th Goal: 27-03-04
Chelsea
vs Wolverhampton
Wanderers 77th min

DIDIER DROGBA 220 Games

100th Goal: 10-03-12
Chelsea
vs Stoke City
68th min

DARREN BENT 226 Games

100th Goal: 01-02-12
Aston Villa
vs QPR
45th min

WAYNE ROONEY 247 Games

100th Goal: 31-01-10
Manchester United
vs Arsenal
37th min

DWIGHT YORKE 254 Games

100th Goal: 25-11-00
Manchester United
vs Derby County
76th min

Alan Shearer's record may never be beaten, but he is not the record holder for English top-flight football. That honour goes to a Scotsman, Dave Halliday, who signed for Sunderland from Dundee in 1925. In the old Division One, Halliday hit 100 goals in just 101 games. To this day he is still the only player in top-flight football in England to score more than 30 goals in four consecutive seasons.

TEDDY SHERINGHAM 254 Games

100th Goal: 28-10-00
Manchester United
vs Southampton
51st min

ROBBIE KEANE 255 Games

100th Goal: 26-12-07
Tottenham Hotspur
vs Fulham
62nd min

NICOLAS ANELKA 258 Games

100th Goal: 14-12-08
Chelsea
vs West Ham United
51st min

MATT LE TISSIER 266 Games

100th Goal: 02-04-01
Southampton
vs Arsenal
89th min

DION DUBLIN 271 Games

100th Goal: 23-11-02
Aston Villa
vs West Ham United
71st min

JERMAIN DEFOE 303 Games

100th Goal: 23-04-11
Tottenham Hotspur vs West Bromwich Albion
66th min

FRANK LAMPARD 406 Games

100th Goal: 01-11-08
Chelsea
vs Sunderland
51st min

EMILE HESKEY 414 Games

100th Goal: 01-11-08
Wigan Athletic
vs Portsmouth
90th min

PETER CROUCH 419 Games

100th Goal: 01-02-17
Stoke City
vs Everton
7th min

PAUL SCHOLES 436 Games

100th Goal: 06-03-10
Manchester United
vs Wolverhampton
Wanderers, 72nd min

STEVEN GERRARD 449 Games

100th Goal: 19-10-13
Liverpool
vs Newcastle United
42nd min

RYAN GIGGS 534 Games

100th Goal 28-11-2009
Manchester United
vs Portsmouth
87th min

CONCACAF GOLD CUP RECORDS BY NATION

The CONCACAF Gold Cup is a biennial competition for nations from North and Central America and the Caribbean. The six-team tournament was first held in 1963 and then every two years. Between 1973 and 1989, the competition was held every four years and doubled as a World Cup qualifying process. In 1991 it was expanded to eight teams and reverted to a biennial format and in 2001 it was enlarged to 12 nations. Between 1997 and 2003 guest teams, including Brazil and Colombia, also competed in the tournament. The next CONCACAF Gold Cup is to be hosted by the USA in July 2017.

QUALIFICATION NOTES
The colour coding and winners and hosts icons are based only on the Gold Cup since 1991.

Mexico have won the CONCACAF Gold Cup a record ten times.

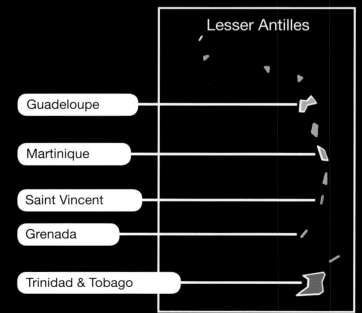

Lesser Antilles

Guadeloupe

Martinique

Saint Vincent

Grenada

Trinidad & Tobago

Canada

Winner
Host

Qualified
0
1
2
3
4
5
6
7
8
9
10
11
12
13

Source: FIFA (Octob...

United States of America

Mexico

Cuba

Jamaica

Belize

Honduras

Haiti

Guatemala

Nicaragua

El Salvador

Panama

Costa Rica

Also competed: Brazil (3),
Colombia (3), Korea Republic
(2), Ecuador (1), Peru (1),
South Africa (1).

FA CUP WINNERS AND RUNNERS-UP

Although overshadowed in recent times by the Premier League, the FA Cup remains the showpiece of English football. First played in the 1871–72 season, the English FA Cup is the oldest football competition in the world. Open to the top 10 levels of English football, the tournament includes hundreds of non-league teams (in 1901, Tottenham Hotspur became the only non-league team ever to win the trophy). Since 1923, the final has been played at Wembley (old and new) apart from the period between 2001 and 2006, when it was hosted at the Millennium Stadium in Cardiff.

Source: Opta (May 2017)

PERCENTAGE OF FINALS WON

BURY — 1900 · 1903

WANDERERS — 1872 · 1878 — 1872, 1873, 1876, 1877, 1878

TOTTENHAM HOTSPUR — 1901 · 1991 — 1901, 1921, 1961, 1962, 1967, 1981, 1982, 1987, 1991

BLACKBURN ROVERS — 1884 · 1928 — 1882, 1884, 1885, 1886, 1890, 1891, 1928, 1960

BLACKBURN OLYMPIC — 1883
BRADFORD CITY — 1911
COVENTRY CITY — 1987
IPSWICH TOWN — 1978
OLD CARTHUSIANS — 1881
WIGAN ATHLETIC — 2013
WIMBLEDON — 1988

NOTTINGHAM FOREST — 1898 · 1959 — 1898, 1959, 1991

SHEFFIELD UNITED — 1899 · 1925 — 1901, 1902, 1915, 1925, 1936

WEST HAM UNITED — 1964 · 1980 — 1923, 1964, 1975, 1980, 2006

BOLTON WANDERERS — 1923 · 1958

MANCHESTER CITY — 1904 · 2011 — 2011, 2013

WEST BROMWICH ALBION — 1888 · 1968 — 1886, 1888, 1892, 1895, 1912, 1931, 1935, 1954, 1968

SUNDERLAND — 1937 · 1973 — 1913, 1937, 1973, 1992

SHEFFIELD WEDNESDAY — 1896 · 1935 — 1890, 1896, 1900, 1907, 1935, 1966, 1993

WOLVERHAMPTON WANDERERS — 1893 · 1960 — 1889, 1893, 1896, 1908, 1921, 1939, 1949, 1960

BARNSLEY — 1910, 1912
CHARLTON ATHLETIC — 1946, 1947
CLAPHAM ROVERS — 1879, 1880
NOTTS COUNTY — 1891, 1894

PORTSMOUTH — 1939 · 2008 — 1929, 1934, 1939, 2008, 2010

OLD ETONIANS — 1879 · 1882 — 1875, 1876, 1879, 1881, 1882, 1883

PRESTON NORTH END — 1889 · 1938 — 1888, 1889, 1922, 1937, 1938, 1954, 1964

BLACKPOOL — 1948, 1951, 1953
BURNLEY — 1914, 1947, 1962
CARDIFF CITY — 1925, 1927, 2008

HUDDERSFIELD TOWN — 1920, 1922, 1928, 1930, 1938

Brighton and Hove Albion — 1983
Bristol City — 1909
Fulham — 1975
Hull City — 2014
Luton Town — 1959
Middlesbrough — 1997
Millwall — 2004
Queens Park Rangers — 1982
Stoke City — 2011
Watford — 1984

DERBY COUNTY — 1898, 1899, 1903, 1946
LEEDS UNITED — 1965, 1970, 1972, 1973
OXFORD UNIVERSITY — 1873, 1874, 1877, 1880
ROYAL ENGINEERS — 1872, 1874, 1875, 1878
SOUTHAMPTON — 1900, 1902, 1976, 2003

Birmingham City — 1931, 1956
Crystal Palace — 1990, 2016
Queen's Park (Glasgow) — 1884, 1885

Leicester City — 1949, 1961, 1963, 1969

NUMBER OF APPEARANCES IN THE FA CUP FINAL

Among the many gems of FA Cup trivia are that Wigan Athletic are the only club to win the FA Cup and be relegated from the Premier League in the same season (2013); Leicester City have reached the final four times but have never won the cup; and Ashley Cole holds a record seven FA Cup winner's medals through his victories with Arsenal and Chelsea.

TEAM NAME

Year of first win

Year of last win

XXXX · XXXX

Final appearances

Total number of final wins

Total number of final runners-up finishes

WIGAN ATHLETIC

2013 ↓

LEICESTER CITY

0 | 4

ASHLEY COLE

Y Y Y Y Y Y Y

11 12 13 14 15 16 17 18 19 20

90

80

ASTON VILLA
1887 · 1957

CHELSEA
1970 · 2012

NEWCASTLE UNITED
1910 · 1955

LIVERPOOL
1965 · 2006

EVERTON
1906 · 1995

MANCHESTER UNITED
1909 · 2016

ARSENAL
1930 · 2017

40

30

20

10

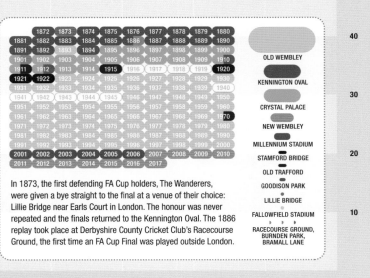

	1872	1873	1874	1875	1876	1877	1878	1879	1880
1881	1882	1883	1884	1885	1886	1887	1888	1889	1890
1891	1892	1893	1894	1895	1896	1897	1898	1899	1900
1901	1902	1903	1904	1905	1906	1907	1908	1909	1910
1911	1912	1913	1914	1915	1916	1917	1918	1919	1920
1921	1922	1923	1924	1925	1926	1927	1928	1929	1930
1931	1932	1933	1934	1935	1936	1937	1938	1939	1940
1941	1942	1943	1944	1945	1946	1947	1948	1949	1950
1951	1952	1953	1954	1955	1956	1957	1958	1959	1960
1961	1962	1963	1964	1965	1966	1967	1968	1969	1970
1971	1972	1973	1974	1975	1976	1977	1978	1979	1980
1981	1982	1983	1984	1985	1986	1987	1988	1989	1990
1991	1992	1993	1994	1995	1996	1997	1998	1999	2000
2001	2002	2003	2004	2005	2006	2007	2008	2009	2010
2011	2012	2013	2014	2015	2016	2017			

OLD WEMBLEY

KENNINGTON OVAL

CRYSTAL PALACE

NEW WEMBLEY

MILLENNIUM STADIUM

STAMFORD BRIDGE

OLD TRAFFORD

GOODISON PARK

LILLIE BRIDGE

FALLOWFIELD STADIUM

RACECOURSE GROUND, BURNDEN PARK, BRAMALL LANE

In 1873, the first defending FA Cup holders, The Wanderers, were given a bye straight to the final at a venue of their choice: Lillie Bridge near Earls Court in London. The honour was never repeated and the finals returned to the Kennington Oval. The 1886 replay took place at Derbyshire County Cricket Club's Racecourse Ground, the first time an FA Cup Final was played outside London.

11 12 13 14 15 16 17 18 19 20

1986 WORLD CUP GOALS

Mexico may have hosted the 1986 World Cup, but the tournament was all about one man – Argentina's Diego Maradona. The 25-year-old's goals against England and Belgium were described by many pundits, players and fans alike as "pure genius". In the now famous quarter-final match against England, Maradona's unforgettable "Hand of God" goal was (almost) forgotten when he scored his "Goal of the Century" just four minutes later. His achievements would dwarf the World Cup's other magical moments, which included six goals from England's Gary Lineker (the tournament's top scorer), a screamer from Brazil's Josimar and an ambitious scissor-kick from the Mexican player Manuel Negrete.

DIEGO MARADONA – Argentina vs England

Diego Maradona dribbles the ball beyond England goalkeeper Peter Shilton to score the "Goal of the Century". Argentina won 2–1, 22 June 1986.

1. Pass **Hoddle**
2. Pass **Brown**
3. Ball recovery **Brown**
4. Pass **Enrique**
5. Take on **Maradona**
6. Challenge **Reid**
7. Take on **Maradona**
8. Challenge **Butcher**
9. Take on **Maradona**
10. Challenge **Fenwick**
11. Take on **Maradona**
12. Challenge **Shilton**
13. Goal **Maradona**

KEY

Ball movement	▬▬▬	Player with ball	▪▪▪▪▪▪▪▪▪▪
Shot	▬▬⚽	Player without ball	•••••••••••

CARECA – Brazil vs France

1. Keeper pick-up **Bats**
2. Keeper kick from hands (long ball) **Bats**
3. Clearance **César**
4. Ball recovery **Josimar**
5. Pass (chipped) **Josimar**
6. Pass **Sócrates**
7. Pass **Alemão**
8. Pass **Josimar**
9. Pass **Sócrates**
10. Pass **Müller**
11. Pass **Müller**
12. Pass **Júnior**
13. Goal **Careca**

MICHAEL LAUDRUP – Denmark vs Uruguay

GARY LINEKER – England vs Poland

1. Pass (chipped, long ball) **Wójcicki**
2. Ball recovery **Sansom**
3. Pass **Sansom**
4. Pass **Shilton**
5. Pass **Reid**
6. Pass **Butcher**
7. Pass **Sansom**
8. Pass **Beardsley**
9. Pass (cross, long ball) **Hodge**
10. Goal **Lineker**

JEAN TIGANA – France vs Hungary

EUROPEAN CHAMPIONSHIP TROPHIES AND GOALS

It's an old football cliché, but it is certainly true that there have been no easy games in the European Championship. The format of this much-revered event has historically led to a select and elite group of nations reaching the finals, so this data is not distorted by easy wins and goal feasts. While Germany are top in the all-time Euro table, the other leading nations have similar records – except for England, whose lack of success in the competition is starkly obvious.

GERMANY
72
26
3

FRANCE
62
20
2

NETHERLANDS
57
17
1

SPAIN
55
19
3

PORTUGAL
49
18
1

ENGLAND
40
10

ITALY
39
16
1

CZECH REPUBLIC
30
10

DENMARK 30 / 7 / 1

SWEDEN 25 / 5

CROATIA 23 / 8

BELGIUM 22 / 7

YUGOSLAVIA 22 / 3

RUSSIA 20 / 5

USSR 17 / 7 / 1

GREECE 14 / 5 / 1

TURKEY 13 / 4

CZECHOSLOVAKIA 12 / 3 / 1

HUNGARY 11 / 2

ROMANIA 10 / 1

WALES 10 / 4

ICELAND 8 / 2

SWITZERLAND 8 / 2

POLAND 7 / 2

REPUBLIC OF IRELAND 6 / 2

BULGARIA 4 / 1

SCOTLAND 4 / 2

SLOVENIA 4

SLOVAKIA 3 / 1

AUSTRIA 2

NORTHERN IRELAND 2 / 1

UKRAINE 2 / 1

ALBANIA 1 / 1

CIS 1

LATVIA 1

NORWAY 1 / 1

● **TOURNAMENTS WON**
● **MATCHES WON**
● **GOALS SCORED**

Source: Opta (July 2016)

73

UEFA CHAMPIONS LEAGUE DECADE-BY-DECADE PERFORMANCE

England remains the supplier of the biggest number of clubs to reach the semi-finals of the European Cup and Champions League. Ten teams from the English league have made the final four – Manchester United (12 times), Liverpool (9), Chelsea (7), Leeds United (3), Arsenal (2), Nottingham Forest (2), Derby County (1), Manchester City (1), Tottenham Hotspur (1) and Aston Villa (1). France and Germany have provided eight different clubs, while seven Spanish clubs, six different Italian teams and five Scottish have also made the final hurdle.

| 1950s | 1960s | 1970s | 1980s |

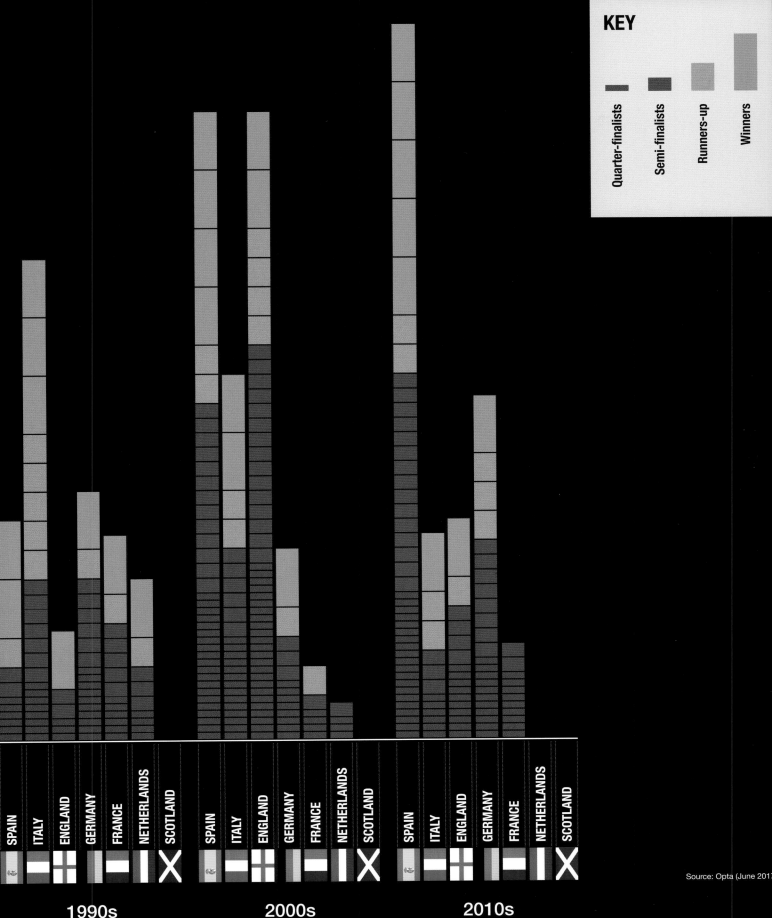

Quarter-finalists

Semi-finalists

Runners-up

Winners

SPAIN

ITALY

ENGLAND

GERMANY

FRANCE

NETHERLANDS

SCOTLAND

SPAIN

ITALY

ENGLAND

GERMANY

FRANCE

NETHERLANDS

SCOTLAND

SPAIN

ITALY

ENGLAND

GERMANY

FRANCE

NETHERLANDS

SCOTLAND

1990s

2000s

2010s

Source: Opta (June 2017)

FIFA WORLD CUP WINS BY COUNTRY

Brazil truly are the World Cup kings. Not only are they the most successful nation, they also top the chart of World Cup wins, have registered the most consecutive wins (from 2002 vs Turkey to 2006 vs Ghana) and they are the only team to have won all their matches in two tournaments (1970 and 2002). At the other end of the scale, Bulgaria failed to win in five finals from 1962 to 1986, before finally beating Greece in their second game in 1994.

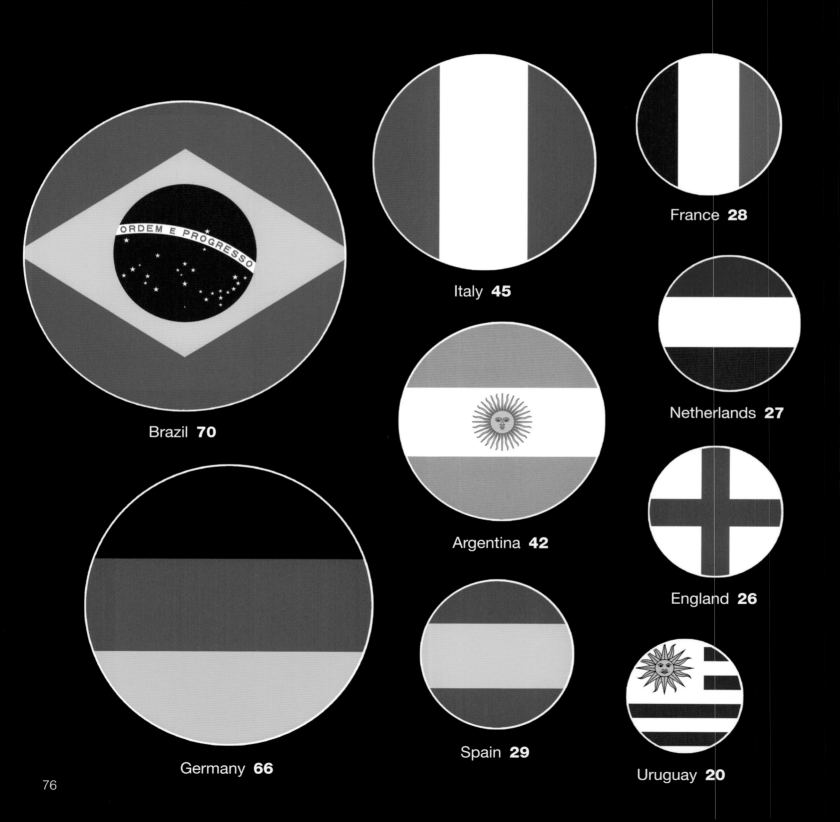

Italy **45**

France **28**

Netherlands **27**

Brazil **70**

Argentina **42**

England **26**

Germany **66**

Spain **29**

Uruguay **20**

Source: Opta (August 2015)
Data relates to individual games won per team, 1930–2014

Yugoslavia **16**

Belgium **14**

Denmark **8**

Nigeria **5**

Northern Ireland **3**

East Germany **2**

Czech Republic **1**

Sweden **16**

Mexico **14**

Romania **8**

Peru **4**

Greece **2**

Tunisia **1**

Hungary **15**

Portugal **13**

USA **8**

Ghana **4**

Morocco **2**

Jamaica **1**

Poland **15**

Austria **12**

Colombia **7**

Japan **4**

Ukraine **2**

Slovenia **1**

USSR **15**

Chile **11**

Croatia **7**

Republic of Ireland **2**

Bosnia and Herzegovina **1**

Switzerland **11**

Paraguay **7**

Ecuador **4**

Senegal **2**

DPR Korea **1**

Czechoslovakia **11**

Costa Rica **5**

Scotland **4**

Saudi Arabia **2**

Cuba **1**

Turkey **5**

Cameroon **4**

Russia **2**

Iran **1**

Korea Republic **5**

Algeria **3**

Norway **2**

Slovakia **1**

Ivory Coast **3**

Australia **2**

Wales **1**

Bulgaria **3**

South Africa **2**

Serbia **1**

77

EREDIVISIE GAME WINS

Ajax, Feyenoord and PSV have been the dominant Eredivisie clubs, with all three having many successful spells – often sharing the limelight with the others. PSV had the Romario-inspired team around 1990 and Gus Hiddink's all-conquering side in the early 2000s. Feyenoord's 1971 European Cup side boasted the talents of Willem van Hanegem and winger Coen Moulijn, and Ajax have consistently competed for the title, reaching almost unsurpassable heights with the 1970s team of Johan Neeskens and Johan Cruyff and the '90s line-ups including Dennis Bergkamp, Patrick Kluivert, Edgar Davids and Clarence Seedorf.

Club	Wins
FC AMSTERDAM	61
BLAUW-WIT	65
ELINKWIJK	65
RAPID JC HEERLEN	73
FC DEN BOSCH	114
TELSTAR	118
SC ENSCHEDE	121
GVAV	123
FORTUNA '54 GELEEN	141
DWS	147
EXCELSIOR	148
DE GRAAFSCHAP	149
PEC ZWOLLE	157
HERACLES ALMELO	167
DOS UTRECHT	168
HAARLEM	172
FORTUNA SITTARD	179
VVV-VENLO	189
FC VOLENDAM	228
RKC WAALWIJK	240
GO AHEAD EAGLES	325
MVV MAASTRICHT	350
SC HEERENVEEN	351
N.E.C.	379
VITESSE	418
WILLEM II	420
FC GRONINGEN	443
ADO DEN HAAG	476
NAC BREDA	515

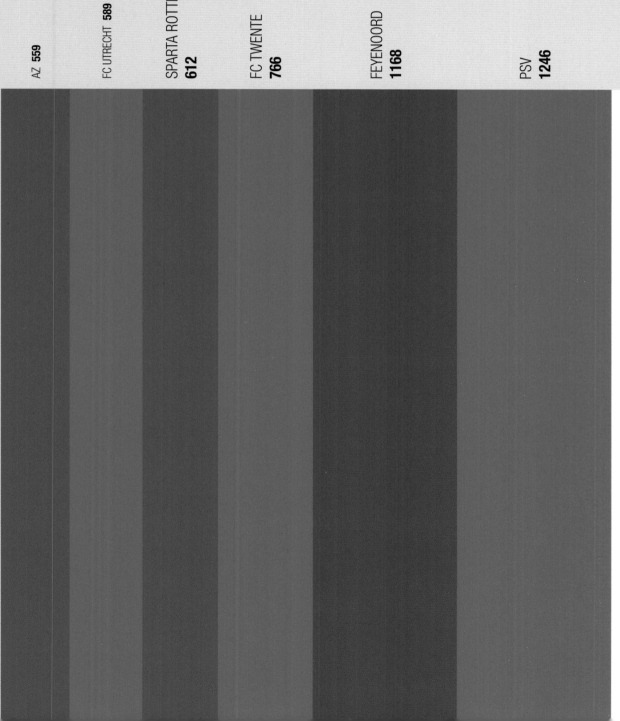

Source: Opta (May 2017)

Under 50 Wins

SC CAMBUUR **49**	XERXESDZB **26**	WAGENINGEN **13**
SHS **37**	FC EINDHOVEN **23**	HELMOND SPORT **12**
RBC ROOSENDAAL **35**	BVC AMSTERDAM **20**	VEENDAM **12**
NOAD **33**	BVV **18**	ALKMAAR **6**
SITTARDIA **32**	DE VOLEWIJCKERS **15**	
FC DORDRECHT **31**	SVV **13**	

RODA JC KERKRADE **555**

AZ **559**

FC UTRECHT **589**

SPARTA ROTTERDAM **612**

FC TWENTE **766**

FEYENOORD **1168**

PSV **1246**

AJAX **1360**

PREMIER LEAGUE GAME WINS

The Premier League thrives on the ability of any of its teams to beat another. Although the elite teams generally dominate the top of the table, they cannot be sure of winning every game. The league winners collect around 27 wins in a season, Chelsea holding the record with 30 wins (2016–17). Consecutive runs of eight or more victories are rare, Arsenal setting the bar at 14 in 2002.

Source: Opta (May 2017)

Team	Wins
IPSWICH TOWN	57
NOTTINGHAM FOREST	60
DERBY COUNTY	68
BIRMINGHAM CITY	73
SWANSEA CITY	74
PORTSMOUTH	79
QUEENS PARK RANGERS	81
WIGAN ATHLETIC	85
CRYSTAL PALACE	86
NORWICH CITY	89
CHARLTON ATHLETIC	93
WIMBLEDON	99
COVENTRY CITY	99
SHEFFIELD WEDNESDAY	101
WEST BROMWICH ALBION	106
STOKE CITY	109
LEICESTER CITY	130
BOLTON WANDERERS	149
FULHAM	150
SUNDERLAND	138
MIDDLESBROUGH	165
LEEDS UNITED	189
SOUTHAMPTON	222
BLACKBURN ROVERS	262
WEST HAM UNITED	265
ASTON VILLA	316

Under 50 Wins

HULL CITY **41**	OLDHAM ATHLETIC **22**
WATFORD **34**	BRADFORD CITY **14**
WOLVERHAMPTON WANDERERS **32**	BLACKPOOL **10**
READING **32**	BARNSLEY **10**
SHEFFIELD UNITED **32**	CARDIFF CITY **7**
BURNLEY **26**	SWINDON TOWN **5**
BOURNEMOUTH **23**	

NEWCASTLE UNITED **322**

MANCHESTER CITY **327**

EVERTON **349**

TOTTENHAM HOTSPUR **400**

LIVERPOOL **478**

CHELSEA **516**

ARSENAL **525**

MANCHESTER UNITED **604**

FOOTBALL RIVALRIES: PART 2

"The Derby" is an unofficial competition recognized across the football world. It signifies a two-match battle between two rival teams each season, where the victorious side wins hometown pride and temporary bragging rights over the other. Italy plays host to some of the sport's more heated rivalries, the oldest being the *Derby della Lanterna* in which Genoa duel Sampdoria, while *Derby d'Italia* brings together Internazionale Milano and Juventus. Meanwhile, in Spain's La Liga, the dominance of powerhouses Barcelona and Real Madrid has fired *El Clásico*, a rivalry constantly simmering through decades of interconnected history, politics and geography.

| REAL MADRID | VS | BARCELONA |

First Game – Real Madrid 2–1 Barcelona   17-02-1929
TOTAL MATCHES 174

72
69
33

| BARCELONA | VS | ESPANYOL |

First Game – Barcelona 1–0 Espanyol   07-04-1929
TOTAL MATCHES 166

34
96
36

| REAL MADRID | VS | ATLÉTICO MADRID |

First Game – Real Madrid 2–1 Atlético Madrid   24-02-1929
TOTAL MATCHES 160

39
86
35

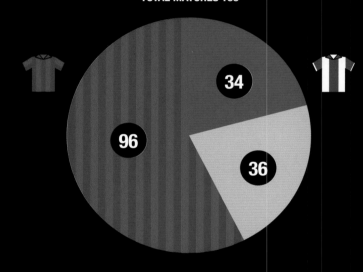

" There is no way to explain it. You have to be inside the game to feel it. The excitement is in knowing that the world practically stops to see you play – and that is priceless."

Real Madrid's Marcelo on *El Clásico*

INTERNAZIONALE MILANO	VS	JUVENTUS

First Game – Internazionale Milano 2–1 Juventus   02-02-1930
TOTAL MATCHES 168

INTERNAZIONALE MILANO	VS	AC MILAN

First Game – Internazionale Milano 2–1 AC Milan   10-11-1929
TOTAL MATCHES 166

SS LAZIO	VS	AS ROMA

First Game – AS Roma 1–0 SS Lazio   08-12-1929
TOTAL MATCHES 146

JUVENTUS	VS	TORINO FC

First Game – Juventus 0–0 Torino FC   24-11-1929
TOTAL MATCHES 144

GENOA	VS	UC SAMPDORIA

First Game – Genoa 2–1 UC Sampdoria   06-10-1935
TOTAL MATCHES 68

Source: Opta (May 2017)

FIFA WORLD PLAYER OF THE YEAR WINNERS

In 2010, the Ballon d'Or merged with FIFA's World Footballer of the Year award, the two competitions having run concurrently since 1991. The Ballon d'Or (Golden Ball) is the award given to the footballer rated by FIFA as the best player in the world. The coach, team captain and a media representative of every nation selects their top three players (awarded five, three and one point, respectively) from a 23-man shortlist devised by FIFA. The top three players in the world are decided by combining all of the points awarded.

LIONEL MESSI (2009, 2010, 2011, 2012, 2015)

CRISTIANO RONALDO (2008, 2013, 2014, 2016)

ZINEDINE ZIDANE (1998, 2000, 2003)

RONALDO (1996, 1997, 2002)

RONALDINHO (2004, 2005)

KAKÁ (2007)

FABIO CANNAVARO (2006)

LUÍS FIGO (2001)

RIVALDO (1999)

GEORGE WEAH (1995)

ROMÁRIO (1994)

ROBERTO BAGGIO (1993)

MARCO VAN BASTEN (1992)

LOTHAR MATTHÄUS (1991)

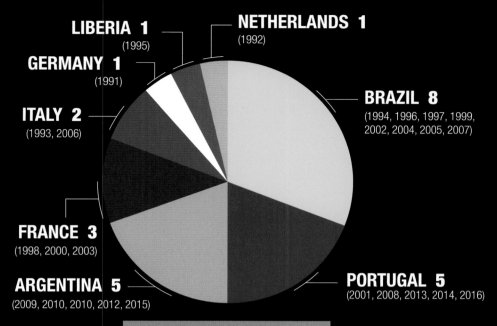

LIBERIA 1
(1995)

GERMANY 1
(1991)

ITALY 2
(1993, 2006)

FRANCE 3
(1998, 2000, 2003)

ARGENTINA 5
(2009, 2010, 2010, 2012, 2015)

NETHERLANDS 1
(1992)

BRAZIL 8
(1994, 1996, 1997, 1999,
2002, 2004, 2005, 2007)

PORTUGAL 5
(2001, 2008, 2013, 2014, 2016)

BY NATION

**"The only bad thing about
Ronaldo's life is Messi.
If it was not for him,
Ronaldo would be the
best player in the world
for five years in a row."**

Filipe Scolari (former coach of Portugal)

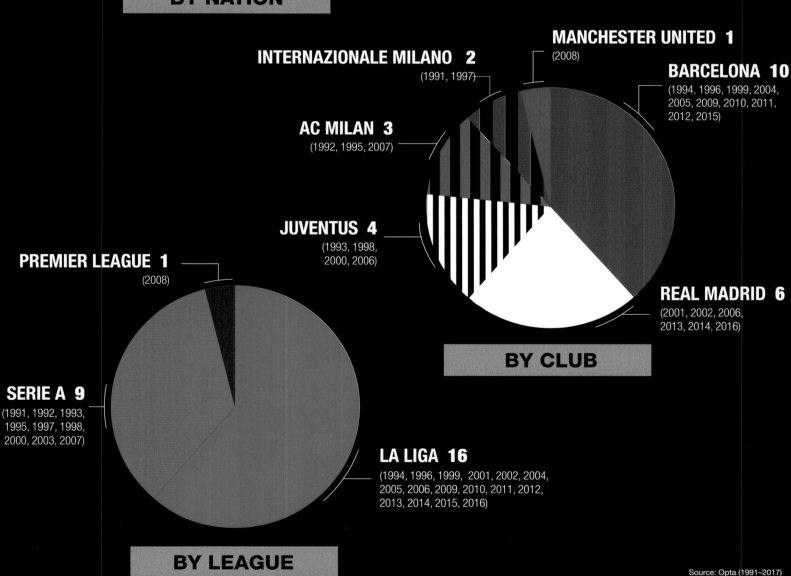

INTERNAZIONALE MILANO 2
(1991, 1997)

AC MILAN 3
(1992, 1995, 2007)

JUVENTUS 4
(1993, 1998,
2000, 2006)

MANCHESTER UNITED 1
(2008)

BARCELONA 10
(1994, 1996, 1999, 2004,
2005, 2009, 2010, 2011,
2012, 2015)

REAL MADRID 6
(2001, 2002, 2006,
2013, 2014, 2016)

BY CLUB

PREMIER LEAGUE 1
(2008)

SERIE A 9
(1991, 1992, 1993,
1995, 1997, 1998,
2000, 2003, 2007)

LA LIGA 16
(1994, 1996, 1999, 2001, 2002, 2004,
2005, 2006, 2009, 2010, 2011, 2012,
2013, 2014, 2015, 2016)

BY LEAGUE

Source: Opta (1991–2017)

LA LIGA GOALS PER CLUB

The history of La Liga is filled with great coaches whose dynamic team engineering has helped squads amass huge goalscoring tallies – from the bowler-hatted Englishman Fred Penland, whose 1930s' Athletic Bilbao conquered any team that stood before them, to the star-studded era of Miguel Muñoz at Real Madrid in the 1960s and 1970s. Johan Cruyff, and his successor Louis van Gaal, brought success back to Barcelona in the '90s. Leo Beenhakker, Vicente del Bosque and Carlo Ancelotti have brought glory to Real Madrid in recent years, while Frank Rijkaard and Pep Guardiola made Barcelona the most feared team in Europe – though judging by the goal totals between those two teams now, there's still everything to play for...

In the 2011–12 season, *La Liga de los Récords* (The League of the Records), a rampant Real Madrid ripped up the record books. Among their notable achievements was the most league goals in a season, as they racked up an astonishing 121. Real boasted 13 different scorers, with Cristiano Ronaldo leading the list on 46, not so closely followed by Gonzalo Higuaín (22) and Karim Benzema (21).

After scoring in 64 consecutive matches, a 0-0 draw at Osasuna on 19 October 2013 brought to an end Real Madrid's record. Then, in February 2016, Barcelona began a run of their own; at the end of the 2016–17 season they had netted in 50 consecutive games … and counting.

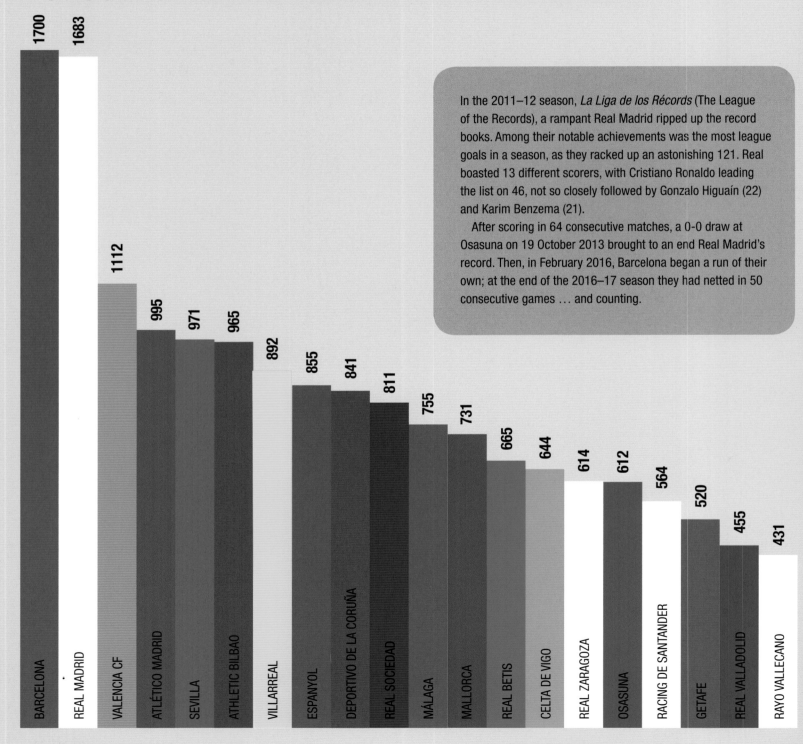

Club	Goals
BARCELONA	1700
REAL MADRID	1683
VALENCIA CF	1112
ATLÉTICO MADRID	995
SEVILLA	971
ATHLETIC BILBAO	965
VILLARREAL	892
ESPANYOL	855
DEPORTIVO DE LA CORUÑA	841
REAL SOCIEDAD	811
MÁLAGA	755
MALLORCA	731
REAL BETIS	665
CELTA DE VIGO	644
REAL ZARAGOZA	614
OSASUNA	612
RACING DE SANTANDER	564
GETAFE	520
REAL VALLADOLID	455
RAYO VALLECANO	431

"MSN", the fearsome Barcelona forward line of Messi, Suárez and Neymar, amassed 79 goals between them in the 2016–17 season.

Source: Opta (May 2017)

LEVANTE **350**
ALAVÉS **290**
ALMERÍA **244**
SPORTING DE GIJÓN **242**
GRANADA CF **209**
LAS PALMAS **180**
RECREATIVO **163**
NUMANCIA **155**
EIBAR **139**
REAL OVIEDO **136**
TENERIFE **113**
ALBACETE **73**
REAL MURCIA **65**
ELCHE **65**
XEREZ **38**
CÁDIZ **36**
HÉRCULES **36**
LEGANÉS **36**
GIMNÀSTIC DE TARRAGONA **34**
SALAMANCA **29**
CF EXTREMADURA **27**
CÓRDOBA **22**

1990 WORLD CUP GOALS

The negativity surrounding the football performances of the 1990 World Cup finals in Italy was alleviated by Luciano Pavarotti's singing of the tournament anthem 'Nessun Dorma', the energy and spirit of Roger Milla and his Cameroon teammates, the passion and drama of England's Paul Gascoigne and the superboots of Italy's Salvatore "Totò" Schillaci. There were outstanding goals galore too, including a surging run and knockout shot from Germany's Lothar Matthäus, an over-the-shoulder volley from England's David Platt and virtuoso brilliance by Italy's one-and-only *Il Divin Codino* (The Divine Ponytail) – Roberto Baggio.

ROBERTO BAGGIO – Italy vs Czechoslovakia

Roberto Baggio on his way to scoring Italy's second goal. Italy won 2–0 against Czechoslovakia, 19 June 1990.

1. Take on **Schillaci**
2. Tackle **Hašek**
3. Pass **Giannini**
4. Pass **Baggio**
5. Pass **Giannini**
6. Take on **Baggio**
7. Challenge **Hašek**
8. Goal **Baggio**

KEY

Ball movement ——————

Shot ——————⚽

Player with ball ⋯⋯⋯⋯⋯⋯

Player without ball ⋯⋯⋯⋯⋯⋯

CLAUDIO CANIGGIA – **Argentina** vs Brazil

1. Pass **Ruggeri**
2. Challenge **Alemão**
3. Take on **Maradona**
4. Take on **Maradona**
5. Challenge **Dunga**
6. Through ball **Maradona**
7. Challenge **Taffarel**
8. Take on **Caniggia**
9. Goal **Caniggia**

LOTHAR MATTHÄUS – **Germany** vs Yugoslavia

1. Challenge **Brehme**
2. Pass **Stojković**
3. Ball recovery **Buchwald**
4. Pass **Buchwald**
5. Pass **Augenthaler**
6. Take on **Matthäus**
7. Challenge **Jozić**
8. Goal **Matthäus**

ROGER MILLA – **Cameroon** vs Romania

1. Dispossesed **Timofte**
2. Tackle **Pagal**
3. Launch (long ball) **Onana**
4. Aerial **Andone**
5. Aerial **Milla**
6. Error **Andone**
7. Goal **Milla**

ENZO SCIFO – **Belgium** vs Uruguay

1. Pass (chipped) **Ostolaza**
2. Clearance **De Wolf**
3. Ball recovery **Gerets**
4. Pass **Gerets**
5. Pass **Van der Elst**
6. Pass **Scifo**
7. Keeper pick-up **Preud'homme**
8. Keeper kick from hands (long ball) **Preud'homme**
9. Clearance **de León**
10. Pass **Ceulemans**
11. Pass **Scifo**
12. Pass **Ceulemans**
13. Pass **Versavel**
14. Pass **Van der Elst**
15. Goal **Scifo**

Source: Opta (October 2015)

STAYING POWER

Promotion to the top league presents a wonderful opportunity to establish a club in the top flight. The lucky ones such as TSG 1899 Hoffenheim in the Bundesliga or AC Monaco in Ligue 1 thrive, usually helped by big money backers. Some, like US Pistoiese 1921 (Serie A, 1980–81) or Barnsley (Premier League, 1998–99), are immediately relegated and never seen again. More often they are "yo-yo" teams like FC Nürnberg, Middlesbrough, Real Betis or FC Bari 1908, doomed to eternally oscillate between promotion and relegation.

2000–01   2001–02   2002–03   2003–04   2004–05   2005–06   2006–07   2007–08   2008–09

ENGLISH PREMIER LEAGUE
ITALIAN SERIE A
GERMAN BUNDESLIGA
FRENCH LIGUE 1
SPANISH LA LIGA

Source: Opta (May 2017)

This anomaly in the data highlights the May 2006 Italian football scandal, where Italian police implicated many Serie A teams' managers and league referees for their creation of a highly organized match-fixing network.

Against all predictions, there is not one occasion in this time period when all promoted teams are immediately relegated the following season.

| | Up | | 5 |
| Down | |

| | Up | | 4 |
| Down | |

| | Up | | 3 |
| Down | |

| | Up | | 2 |
| Down | |

| | Up | | 1 |
| Down | |

| | Up | | 0 |
| Down | |

2009–10 2010–11 2011–12 2012–13 2013–14 2014–15 2015–16 2016–17

UEFA CUP/EUROPA LEAGUE RECORDS BY NATION

The Europa League is UEFA's tournament for the continent's top teams who have failed to qualify for the Champions League, who have won their domestic cup or who have been eliminated in the early stages of the Champions League. It originated as the UEFA Cup in 1971–72 but, since 2009–10, the competition has been known as the UEFA Europa League. It now invites 177 different teams from 54 nations who enter the tournament at different stages. A team reaching the final from the first qualifying round would play a total of 23 matches. Atlético Madrid (2012) and Sevilla (2014) have both won the competition having began their journey in the third qualifying round.

IFK Göteborg 2

Valencia 1

2 Sweden

Atlético Madrid 2

Sevilla 5

Feyenoord 2

Ajax 1

4 Holland

10 Spain

1 PSV Eindhoven

2 Real Madrid

Schalke 04 1

Borussia Mönchengladbach 2

Bayern Munich 1

6 Germany

Porto 2

2 Portugal

Bayer Leverkusen 1

1 Eintracht Frankfurt

Zenit St Petersburg ①

CSKA Moscow ①

Manchester United ①

Russia 2

Chelsea ①

③ Liverpool

Ipswich Town ①

England 7

Tottenham Hotspur ②

Galatasaray ① Turkey 1

① Napoli

③ Juventus

Anderlecht ①

Parma ②

Belgium 1

Italy 9

Internazionale ③

Shakhtar Donetsk ①

Ukraine 1

Coaches with the most UEFA Cup/Europa League wins

3 Giovanni Trapattoni (Juventus 1976–77 and 1992–93, Internazionale 1990–91)
2 Rafael Benítez (Valencia 2003–04, Chelsea 2012–13)
2 Luis Molowny (Real Madrid 1984–85, 1985–86)
2 Juande Ramos (Sevilla 2005–06, 2006–07)

Source: UEFA.com (May 2017)

MLS GOALS PER CLUB

Thierry Henry, Robbie Keane and Didier Drogba have all scored freely in the States, but the record books are topped by home-grown heroes like Landon Donovan, Jeff Cunningham and Chris Wondolowski. The goals recorded here include such gems as the 50-yard run by Metrostars' Clint Mathis to score the 2001 MLS Goal of the Year, the magnificent flick and volley from the Vancouver Whitecaps' Eric Hassli in 2011 and David Villa's exquisite chip from the halfway line for New York City FC in 2017.

Source: mlssoccer.com (October 2016)
Player data: Colour relates to the team for which the player scored the highest number of goals.

Landon Donovan stands alone in MLS history. He is not only the clear all-time leading scorer but is also at the head of the all-time assists list. In 2009 he won the league's MVP award and in 2015 they named the award after him. Outside of short periods with Bayer Leverkusen, Bayern München and Everton, Donovan has spent his whole career in the MLS; four seasons with San Jose Earthquakes (32 goals) and 11 seasons with LA Galaxy (113 goals). Donovan has won the MLS Cup a record six times – twice with the Earthquakes and four times with the Galaxy.

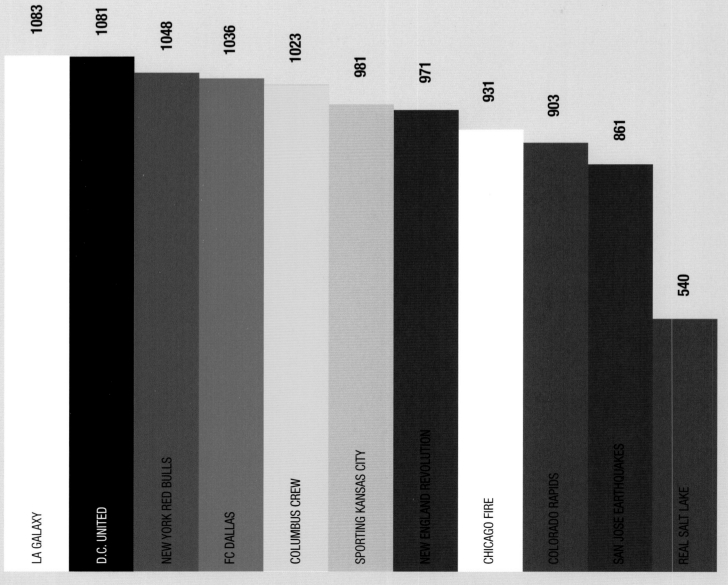

Club	Goals
LA GALAXY	1083
D.C. UNITED	1081
NEW YORK RED BULLS	1048
FC DALLAS	1036
COLUMBUS CREW	1023
SPORTING KANSAS CITY	981
NEW ENGLAND REVOLUTION	971
CHICAGO FIRE	931
COLORADO RAPIDS	903
SAN JOSE EARTHQUAKES	861
REAL SALT LAKE	540

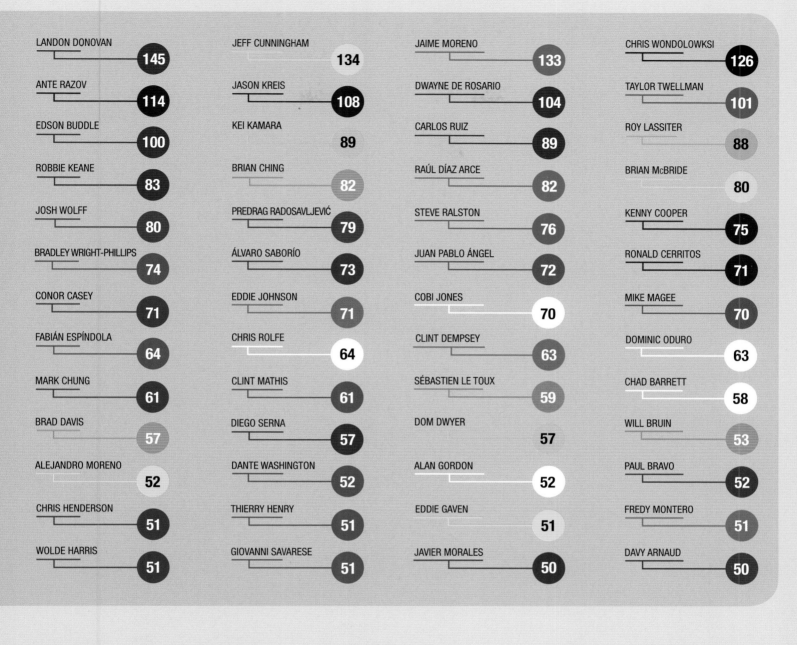

LANDON DONOVAN **145**	JEFF CUNNINGHAM **134**	JAIME MORENO **133**	CHRIS WONDOLOWKSI **126**
ANTE RAZOV **114**	JASON KREIS **108**	DWAYNE DE ROSARIO **104**	TAYLOR TWELLMAN **101**
EDSON BUDDLE **100**	KEI KAMARA **89**	CARLOS RUIZ **89**	ROY LASSITER **88**
ROBBIE KEANE **83**	BRIAN CHING **82**	RAÚL DÍAZ ARCE **82**	BRIAN McBRIDE **80**
JOSH WOLFF **80**	PREDRAG RADOSAVLJEVIĆ **79**	STEVE RALSTON **76**	KENNY COOPER **75**
BRADLEY WRIGHT-PHILLIPS **74**	ÁLVARO SABORÍO **73**	JUAN PABLO ÁNGEL **72**	RONALD CERRITOS **71**
CONOR CASEY **71**	EDDIE JOHNSON **71**	COBI JONES **70**	MIKE MAGEE **70**
FABIÁN ESPÍNDOLA **64**	CHRIS ROLFE **64**	CLINT DEMPSEY **63**	DOMINIC ODURO **63**
MARK CHUNG **61**	CLINT MATHIS **61**	SÉBASTIEN LE TOUX **59**	CHAD BARRETT **58**
BRAD DAVIS **57**	DIEGO SERNA **57**	DOM DWYER **57**	WILL BRUIN **53**
ALEJANDRO MORENO **52**	DANTE WASHINGTON **52**	ALAN GORDON **52**	PAUL BRAVO **52**
CHRIS HENDERSON **51**	THIERRY HENRY **51**	EDDIE GAVEN **51**	FREDY MONTERO **51**
WOLDE HARRIS **51**	GIOVANNI SAVARESE **51**	JAVIER MORALES **50**	DAVY ARNAUD **50**

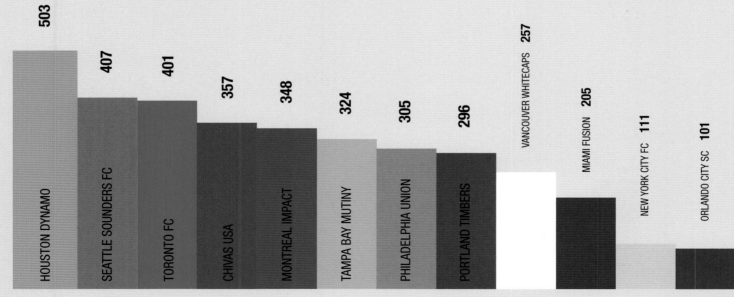

HOUSTON DYNAMO	SEATTLE SOUNDERS FC	TORONTO FC	CHIVAS USA	MONTREAL IMPACT	TAMPA BAY MUTINY	PHILADELPHIA UNION	PORTLAND TIMBERS	VANCOUVER WHITECAPS	MIAMI FUSION	NEW YORK CITY FC	ORLANDO CITY SC
503	407	401	357	348	324	305	296	257	205	111	101

RONALDO vs MESSI

Future generations might well consider us blessed to have seen the two greatest players in the history of the game. Between them they have been named as FIFA's best two players in the world every year since 2008 (except 2010 when Iniesta was runner-up to Messi). Both players have scored in two UEFA Champions League finals, have regularly scored more than 50 goals in a single season, and struck their 500th goals for their club in 2017. But who wouldn't doubt the Argentinian would trade a fair few of them to match the European Championship winner's medal, won by Ronaldo in 2016?

CRISTIANO RONALDO

Club Record

Matches won	**469**
Goals scored	**529**
Games played	**717**

0   800

International Record

Matches won	**84**
Goals scored	**75**
Games played	**142**

0   800

League Championships	🏆🏆🏆🏆🏆
National Cups	🏆🏆🏆
National League Cups	🏆🏆
Comm Shield/Super Cup	🏆🏆🏆
Champions League	🏆🏆🏆🏆
UEFA Super Cup	🏆
Club World Cup	🏆🏆🏆
European Championship	🏆
Total	**21**

> **" Messi is outstanding in certain attributes but Ronaldo is such an all-round player."**
>
> England international Michael Owen

Comm Shield = FA Community Shield / Super Cup = Spanish Super Cup

"Messi or Ronaldo best player in the world? In the world, I would say Ronaldo. Messi is from another planet."

Turkey international Arda Turan

Source: Opta (June 2017)

LIONEL MESSI

Club Record

413	Matches won
507	Goals scored
583	Games played

300   0

International Record

73	Matches won
58	Goals scored
118	Games played

300   0

Trophies	Competition
🏆🏆🏆🏆🏆🏆🏆🏆	League Championships
🏆🏆🏆🏆🏆	National Cups
	National League Cups
🏆🏆🏆🏆🏆🏆	Comm Shield/Super Cup
🏆🏆🏆🏆	Champions League
🏆🏆🏆	UEFA Super Cup
🏆🏆🏆	Club World Cup
🏆	Olympic Gold Medal

30   **Total**

stands today. Played in nine cities across the US, this World Cup saw Italy lose 3–2 to Brazil in a penalty shoot-out – the first ever World Cup final to be decided by penalties. Roberto Baggio's wild penalty miss will long be remembered. The flick, spin and volley by Germany's Jürgen Klinsmann, the 65-yard run to score by Saudi Arabia's Saeed Al-Owairan and the diving header by Bulgaria's Yordan Letchkov were all wonderful goals, but it's Hagi's strike against Colombia that we'll never forget...

GHEORGHE HAGI – Romania vs Colombia

Romania's Gheorghe Hagi celebrates after scoring his unforgettable left foot lob over the top of Colombian keeper Óscar Córdoba, 18 June 1994

1. Tackle **Râducioiu**
2. Ball recovery **Petrescu**
3. Dispossesed **Rincón**
4. Pass **Petrescu**
5. Pass **Popescu**
6. Pass **Munteanu**
7. Goal **Hagi**

KEY

Ball movement	▬▬▬	Player with ball	▪▪▪▪▪▪▪
Shot	▬▬◉	Player without ball	▪▪▪▪▪▪▪

PHILIPPE ALBERT – **Belgium** vs Germany

1. Goal kick (long ball) **Illgner**
2. Aerial **Emmers**
3. Aerial **Buchwald**
4. Head pass **Emmers**
5. Head pass **Boffin**
6. Pass **Albert**
7. Ball recovery **Albert**
8. Lay-off (chipped) **Weber**
9. Pass **Albert**
10. Challenge **Wagner**
11. Pass **Van der Elst**
12. Challenge **Kohler**
13. Take on **Albert**
14. Goal **Albert**

DANIEL AMOKACHI – **Nigeria** vs Greece

1. Pass **Amokachi**
2. Interception **Adepoju**
3. Ball recovery **Emenalo**
4. Pass **Emenalo**
5. Take on **Amokachi**
6. Challenge **Nioplias**
7. Goal **Amokachi**

YORDAN LETCHKOV – **Bulgaria** vs Germany

1. Throw in **Kiriakov**
2. Pass **Kostadinov**
3. Pass **Kiriakov**
4. Take on **Yankov**
5. Challenge **Berthold**
6. Pass (cross, chipped) **Yankov**
7. Goal (head) **Letchkov**

HRISTO STOICHKOV – **Bulgaria** vs Mexico

1. Pass **García**
2. Ball recovery **Yordanov**
3. Pass **Yordanov**
4. Goal **Stoichkov**

Source: Opta (October 2015)

THE FLAIR LEAGUE

We all love a wow moment; those demonstrations of skill that are worth the ticket price alone. When it comes to individuals, EA Sports *FIFA 17* listed its best dribblers as Messi (Barcelona) and Neymar (Barcelona). Real Madrid's Ronaldo tops their most powerful shot list, but the top 10 also includes Hull City's Tom Huddlestone, Schalke's Naldo and Piti from Rayo Vallecano. Take a look at these comparison charts and see where Europe's mazy masters and hot shot kings ply their trade.

Chelsea's often unstoppable Eden Hazard boosted the Premier League's stats by attempting more than 150 dribbles in the 2016–17 season.

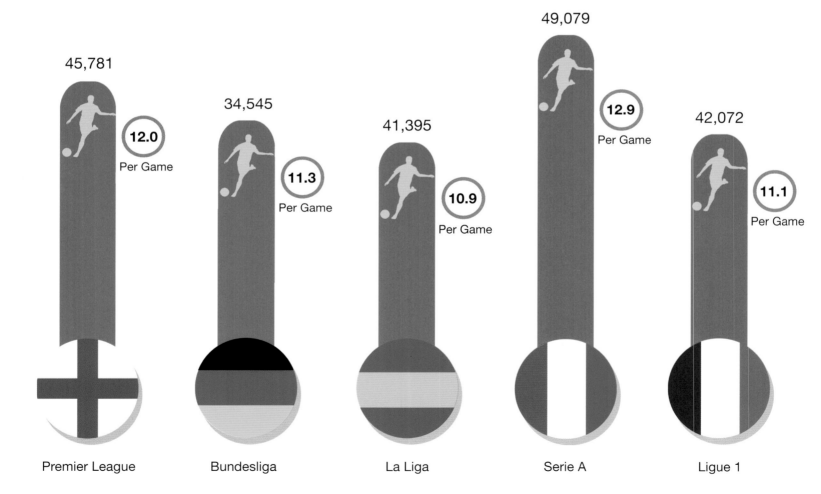

Premier League	Bundesliga	La Liga	Serie A	Ligue 1
45,781	34,545	41,395	49,079	42,072
12.0 Per Game	11.3 Per Game	10.9 Per Game	12.9 Per Game	11.1 Per Game

LONG SHOTS

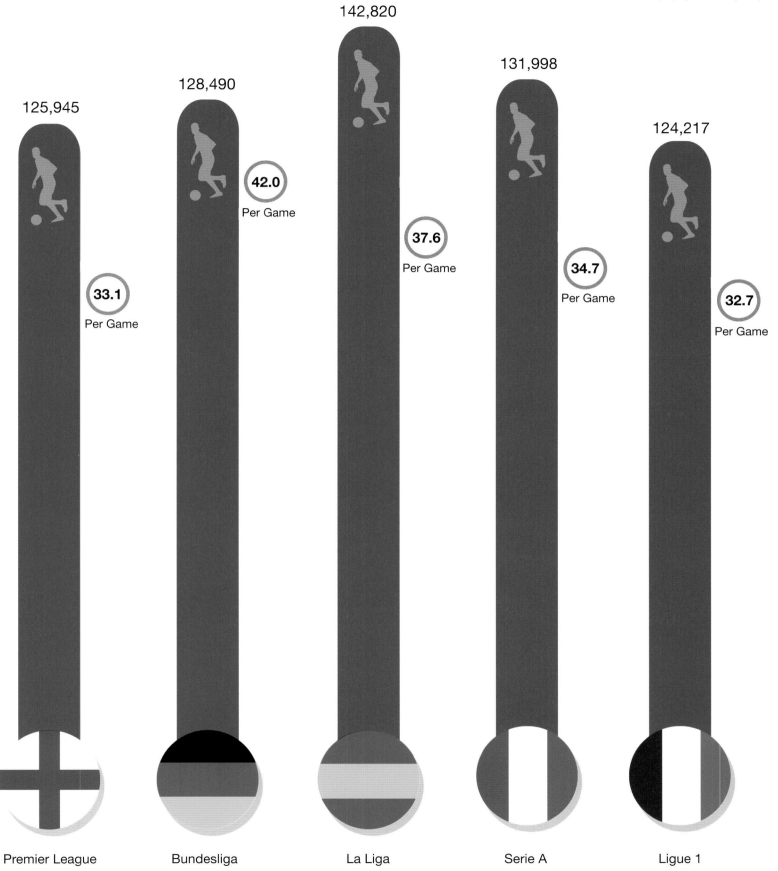

Source: Opta (August 2007–May 2017)

142,820

131,998

128,490

125,945

124,217

42.0
Per Game

37.6
Per Game

34.7
Per Game

33.1
Per Game

32.7
Per Game

Premier League

Bundesliga

La Liga

Serie A

Ligue 1

DRIBBLES

PREMIER LEAGUE PLAYER APPEARANCES

With only 38 Premier League games played a season, a player needs a long career at the highest level to get anywhere near this list. It helps, of course to start young (you'll need at least 12 seasons in the first team), stay injury free and play into your 30s. Even then, it's tough. The youngest to play was Fulham's Matthew Brigg, 16 and 65 days when he made his debut in 2007, he amassed a total of 30 appearances. No wonder only around 100 players have notched up over 300 appearances.

KEY:

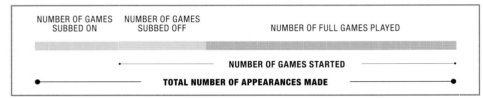

NUMBER OF GAMES SUBBED ON · NUMBER OF GAMES SUBBED OFF · NUMBER OF FULL GAMES PLAYED

NUMBER OF GAMES STARTED

TOTAL NUMBER OF APPEARANCES MADE

* Active up to and including season 2016–17

Source: Opta (May 2017)

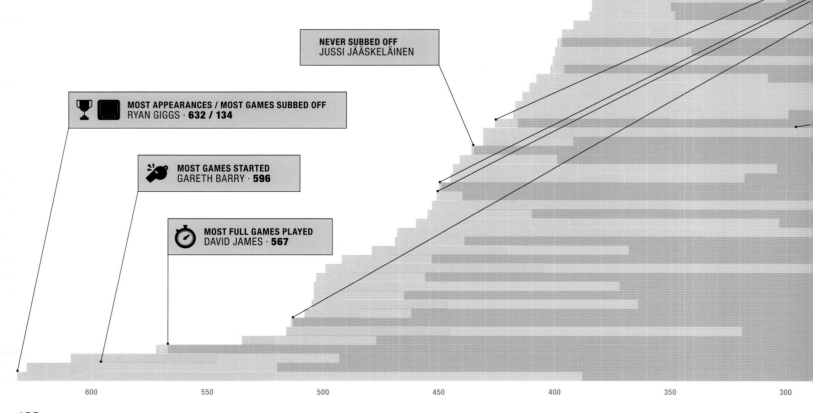

NEVER SUBBED OFF
JUSSI JÄÄSKELÄINEN

MOST APPEARANCES / MOST GAMES SUBBED OFF
RYAN GIGGS · **632 / 134**

MOST GAMES STARTED
GARETH BARRY · **596**

MOST FULL GAMES PLAYED
DAVID JAMES · **567**

600   550   500   450   400   350   300

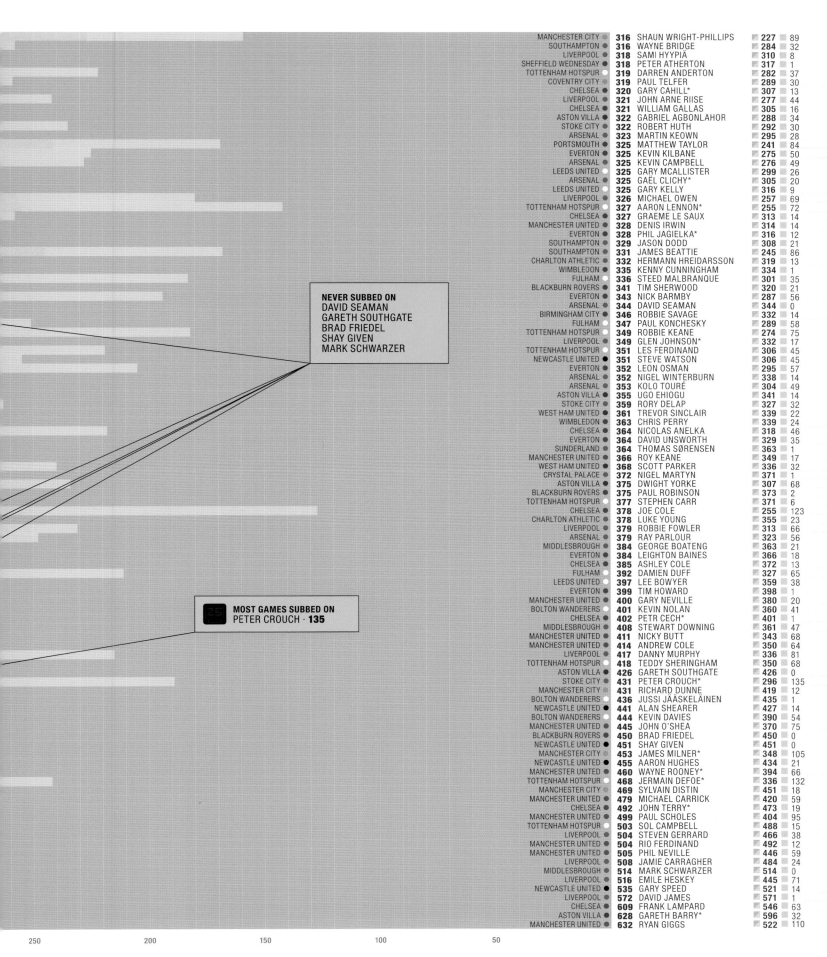

Club		Player		
MANCHESTER CITY ●	316	SHAUN WRIGHT-PHILLIPS	227	89
SOUTHAMPTON ●	316	WAYNE BRIDGE	284	32
LIVERPOOL ●	318	SAMI HYYPIÄ	310	8
SHEFFIELD WEDNESDAY ●	318	PETER ATHERTON	317	1
TOTTENHAM HOTSPUR ○	319	DARREN ANDERTON	282	37
COVENTRY CITY ●	319	PAUL TELFER	289	30
CHELSEA ●	320	GARY CAHILL*	307	13
LIVERPOOL ●	321	JOHN ARNE RIISE	277	44
CHELSEA ●	321	WILLIAM GALLAS	305	16
ASTON VILLA ●	322	GABRIEL AGBONLAHOR	288	34
STOKE CITY ●	322	ROBERT HUTH	292	30
ARSENAL ●	323	MARTIN KEOWN	295	28
PORTSMOUTH ●	325	MATTHEW TAYLOR	241	84
EVERTON ●	325	KEVIN KILBANE	275	50
ARSENAL ●	325	KEVIN CAMPBELL	276	49
LEEDS UNITED ○	325	GARY MCALLISTER	299	26
ARSENAL ●	325	GAËL CLICHY*	305	20
LEEDS UNITED ○	325	GARY KELLY	316	9
LIVERPOOL ●	326	MICHAEL OWEN	257	69
TOTTENHAM HOTSPUR ○	327	AARON LENNON*	255	72
CHELSEA ●	327	GRAEME LE SAUX	313	14
MANCHESTER UNITED ●	328	DENIS IRWIN	314	14
EVERTON ●	328	PHIL JAGIELKA*	316	12
SOUTHAMPTON ●	329	JASON DODD	308	21
SOUTHAMPTON ●	331	JAMES BEATTIE	245	86
CHARLTON ATHLETIC ●	332	HERMANN HREIDARSSON	319	13
WIMBLEDON ●	335	KENNY CUNNINGHAM	334	1
FULHAM ○	336	STEED MALBRANQUE	301	35
BLACKBURN ROVERS ●	341	TIM SHERWOOD	320	21
EVERTON ●	343	NICK BARMBY	287	56
ARSENAL ●	344	DAVID SEAMAN	344	0
BIRMINGHAM CITY ●	346	ROBBIE SAVAGE	332	14
FULHAM ●	347	PAUL KONCHESKY	289	58
TOTTENHAM HOTSPUR ●	349	ROBBIE KEANE	274	75
LIVERPOOL ●	349	GLEN JOHNSON*	332	17
TOTTENHAM HOTSPUR ●	351	LES FERDINAND	306	45
NEWCASTLE UNITED ●	351	STEVE WATSON	306	45
EVERTON ●	352	LEON OSMAN	295	57
ARSENAL ●	352	NIGEL WINTERBURN	338	14
ARSENAL ●	353	KOLO TOURÉ	304	49
ASTON VILLA ●	355	UGO EHIOGU	341	14
STOKE CITY ●	359	RORY DELAP	327	32
WEST HAM UNITED ●	361	TREVOR SINCLAIR	339	22
WIMBLEDON ●	363	CHRIS PERRY	339	14
CHELSEA ●	364	NICOLAS ANELKA	318	46
EVERTON ●	364	DAVID UNSWORTH	329	35
SUNDERLAND ●	364	THOMAS SØRENSEN	363	1
MANCHESTER UNITED ●	366	ROY KEANE	349	17
WEST HAM UNITED ●	368	SCOTT PARKER	336	32
CRYSTAL PALACE ●	372	NIGEL MARTYN	371	1
ASTON VILLA ●	375	DWIGHT YORKE	307	68
BLACKBURN ROVERS ●	375	PAUL ROBINSON	373	2
TOTTENHAM HOTSPUR ○	377	STEPHEN CARR	371	6
CHELSEA ●	378	JOE COLE	255	123
CHARLTON ATHLETIC ●	378	LUKE YOUNG	355	23
LIVERPOOL ●	379	ROBBIE FOWLER	313	66
ARSENAL ●	379	RAY PARLOUR	323	56
MIDDLESBROUGH ●	384	GEORGE BOATENG	363	21
EVERTON ●	384	LEIGHTON BAINES	366	18
CHELSEA ●	385	ASHLEY COLE	372	13
FULHAM ○	392	DAMIEN DUFF	327	65
LEEDS UNITED ○	397	LEE BOWYER	359	38
EVERTON ●	399	TIM HOWARD	398	1
MANCHESTER UNITED ●	400	GARY NEVILLE	380	20
BOLTON WANDERERS ●	401	KEVIN NOLAN	360	41
CHELSEA ●	402	PETR CECH*	401	1
MIDDLESBROUGH ●	408	STEWART DOWNING	361	47
MANCHESTER UNITED ●	411	NICKY BUTT	343	68
MANCHESTER UNITED ●	414	ANDREW COLE	350	64
LIVERPOOL ●	417	DANNY MURPHY	336	81
TOTTENHAM HOTSPUR ●	418	TEDDY SHERINGHAM	350	68
ASTON VILLA ●	426	GARETH SOUTHGATE	426	0
STOKE CITY ●	431	PETER CROUCH*	296	135
MANCHESTER CITY ○	431	RICHARD DUNNE	419	12
BOLTON WANDERERS ○	436	JUSSI JÄÄSKELÄINEN	435	1
NEWCASTLE UNITED ●	441	ALAN SHEARER	427	14
BOLTON WANDERERS ●	444	KEVIN DAVIES	390	54
MANCHESTER UNITED ●	445	JOHN O'SHEA	370	75
BLACKBURN ROVERS ●	450	BRAD FRIEDEL	450	0
NEWCASTLE UNITED ●	451	SHAY GIVEN	451	0
MANCHESTER CITY ○	453	JAMES MILNER*	348	105
NEWCASTLE UNITED ●	455	AARON HUGHES	434	21
MANCHESTER UNITED ●	460	WAYNE ROONEY*	394	66
TOTTENHAM HOTSPUR ○	468	JERMAIN DEFOE*	336	132
MANCHESTER CITY ○	469	SYLVAIN DISTIN	451	18
MANCHESTER UNITED ●	479	MICHAEL CARRICK	420	59
CHELSEA ●	492	JOHN TERRY*	473	19
MANCHESTER UNITED ●	499	PAUL SCHOLES	404	95
TOTTENHAM HOTSPUR ○	503	SOL CAMPBELL	488	15
LIVERPOOL ●	504	STEVEN GERRARD	466	38
MANCHESTER UNITED ●	504	RIO FERDINAND	492	12
MANCHESTER UNITED ●	505	PHIL NEVILLE	446	59
LIVERPOOL ●	508	JAMIE CARRAGHER	484	24
MIDDLESBROUGH ●	514	MARK SCHWARZER	514	0
LIVERPOOL ●	516	EMILE HESKEY	445	71
NEWCASTLE UNITED ●	535	GARY SPEED	521	14
LIVERPOOL ●	572	DAVID JAMES	571	1
CHELSEA ●	609	FRANK LAMPARD	546	63
ASTON VILLA ●	628	GARETH BARRY*	596	32
MANCHESTER UNITED ●	632	RYAN GIGGS	522	110

NEVER SUBBED ON
DAVID SEAMAN
GARETH SOUTHGATE
BRAD FRIEDEL
SHAY GIVEN
MARK SCHWARZER

MOST GAMES SUBBED ON
PETER CROUCH · 135

250   200   150   100   50

PREMIER LEAGUE GOALS PER CLUB

The elite list of Premier League goalscorers changes very slowly – very few of the 100 goal club are still playing. But there are some exceptions. Jermain Defoe moved into the top 10 with his Indian summer at Sunderland, Peter Crouch hit his 100th goal in February 2017 and Sergio Agüero surged up the list with 44 goals in two seasons (2015–16 to 2016–17). Who might be next to join them? The smart money is on Romelu Lukaku (85), Harry Kane (78) or Christian Benteke (66).

> **"Alan Shearer is the greatest English centre-forward there has ever been without a shadow of a doubt; he's a very, very special player. He makes average balls into great balls. He's the scorer of every type of goal going."**
>
> Graeme Souness

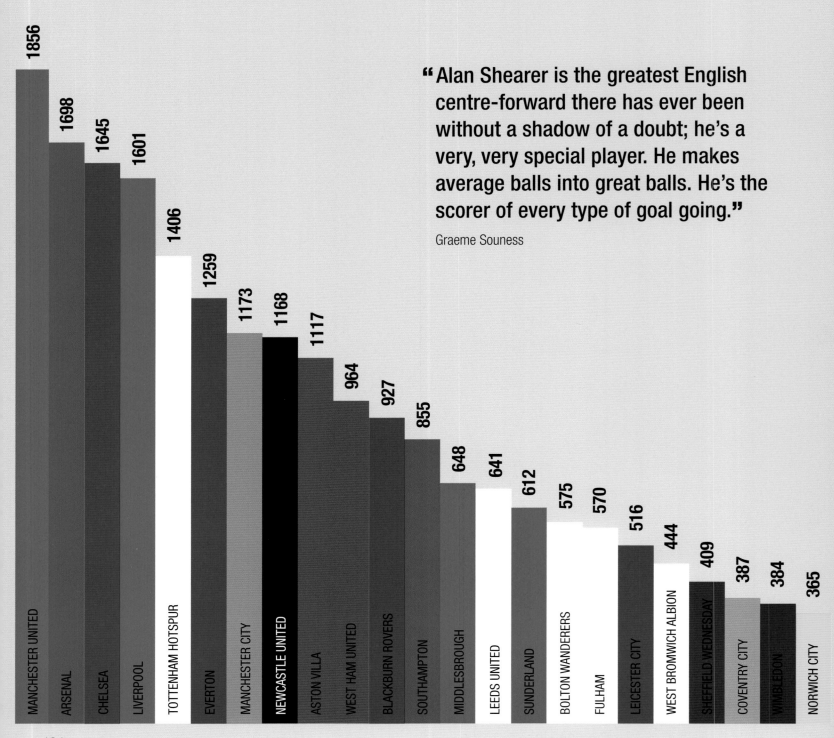

Club	Goals
MANCHESTER UNITED	1856
ARSENAL	1698
CHELSEA	1645
LIVERPOOL	1601
TOTTENHAM HOTSPUR	1406
EVERTON	1259
MANCHESTER CITY	1173
NEWCASTLE UNITED	1168
ASTON VILLA	1117
WEST HAM UNITED	964
BLACKBURN ROVERS	927
SOUTHAMPTON	855
MIDDLESBROUGH	648
LEEDS UNITED	641
SUNDERLAND	612
BOLTON WANDERERS	575
FULHAM	570
LEICESTER CITY	516
WEST BROMWICH ALBION	444
SHEFFIELD WEDNESDAY	409
COVENTRY CITY	387
WIMBLEDON	384
NORWICH CITY	365

ALAN SHEARER	260	WAYNE ROONEY	198	ANDREW COLE	187	FRANK LAMPARD	177

ALAN SHEARER 260
WAYNE ROONEY 198
ANDREW COLE 187
FRANK LAMPARD 177

THIERRY HENRY 175
ROBBIE FOWLER 163
JERMAIN DEFOE 158
MICHAEL OWEN 150

LES FERDINAND 149
TEDDY SHERINGHAM 146
ROBIN VAN PERSIE 144
JIMMY FLOYD HASSELBAINK 127

ROBBIE KEANE 126
NICOLAS ANELKA 125
DWIGHT YORKE 123
SERGIO AGÜERO 122

STEVEN GERRARD 120
IAN WRIGHT 113
DION DUBLIN 111
EMILE HESKEY 110

RYAN GIGGS 109
PAUL SCHOLES 107
DARREN BENT 106
DIDIER DROGBA 104

PETER CROUCH 103
MATTHEW LE TISSIER 100
EMMANUEL ADEBAYOR 97
YAKUBU 95

RUUD VAN NISTELROOY 95
DIMITAR BERBATOV 94
MARK VIDUKA 92
KEVIN PHILLIPS 92

OLE GUNNAR SOLSKJAER 91
JAMES BEATTIE 91
KEVIN DAVIES 88
DENNIS BERGKAMP 87

FERNANDO TORRES 85
LOUIS SAHA 85
ROMELU LUKAKU 85
CARLOS TEVEZ 84

CRISTIANO RONALDO 84
KEVIN CAMPBELL 83
CHRIS SUTTON 83
CRAIG BELLAMY 81

GARY SPEED 80
TONY COTTEE 78
HARRY KANE 78
GABRIEL AGBONLAHOR 74

Source: Opta (May 2017)
Colour relates to the team the player scored the highest number of goals for.

STOKE CITY 363
CHARLTON ATHLETIC 342
QUEENS PARK RANGERS 339
WIGAN ATHLETIC 316
PORTSMOUTH 292
BIRMINGHAM CITY 273
DERBY COUNTY 271
NOTTINGHAM FOREST 229
IPSWICH TOWN 219
HULL CITY 181
WOLVERHAMPTON WANDERERS 156
WATFORD 144
READING 136
SHEFFIELD UNITED 128
BURNLEY 109
OLDHAM ATHLETIC 105
BOURNEMOUTH 100
BRADFORD CITY 68
BLACKPOOL 55
SWINDON TOWN 47
BARNSLEY 37
CARDIFF CITY 32

COPA AMÉRICA TROPHIES AND GOALS

The South American international tournament, Copa América is one of the most intensely fought competitions in world football. There have been 44 (often intermittent) tournaments in the Copa América's 100 years, in which all but Ecuador and Venezuela have been victors. Bolivia's sole victory came on high-altitude home soil in 1963, while Chile contested the most tournaments without a win until 2015, then won again in the centenary competition in 2016. Interestingly, both Pelé and Maradona – and their World Cup-winning teams – failed to secure a Copa América triumph.

ARGENTINA

437
115
14

BRAZIL

398
98
8

URUGUAY

395
107
15

CHILE

270
60
2

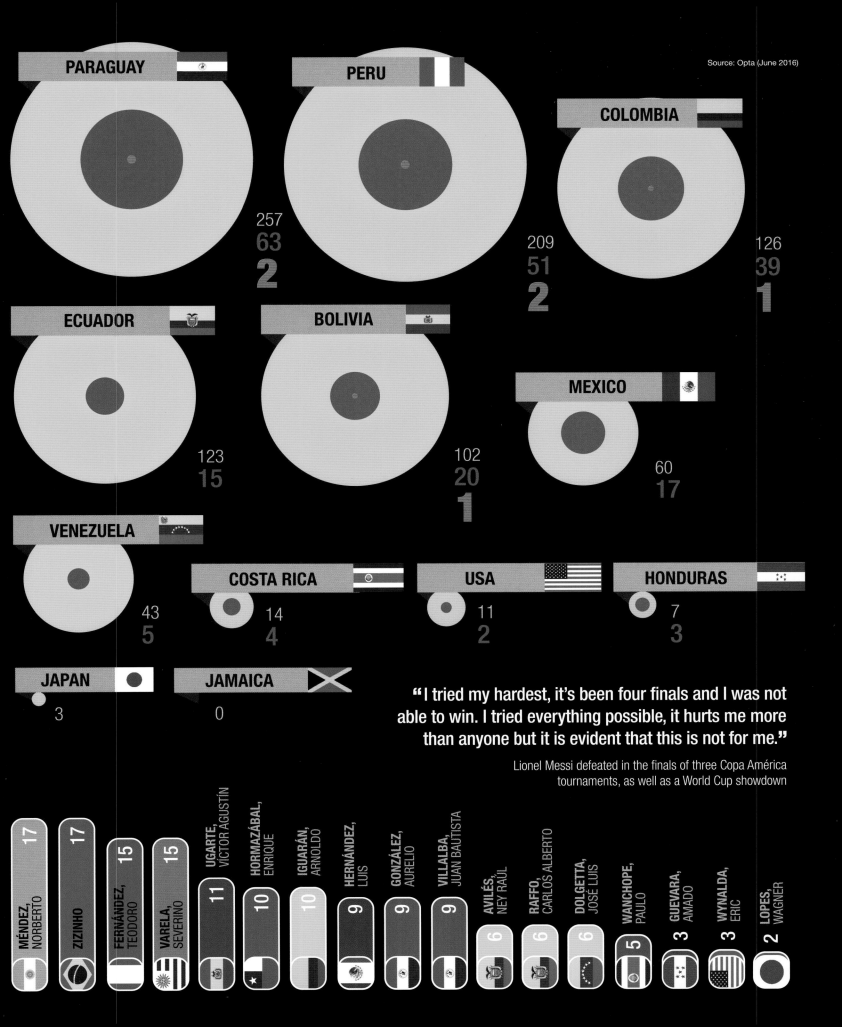

Source: Opta (June 2016)

PARAGUAY
257
63
2

PERU

COLOMBIA
209
51
2
126
39
1

ECUADOR
123
15

BOLIVIA
102
20
1

MEXICO
60
17

VENEZUELA
43
5

COSTA RICA
14
4

USA
11
2

HONDURAS
7
3

JAPAN
3

JAMAICA
0

"I tried my hardest, it's been four finals and I was not able to win. I tried everything possible, it hurts me more than anyone but it is evident that this is not for me."

Lionel Messi defeated in the finals of three Copa América tournaments, as well as a World Cup showdown

MÉNDEZ, NORBERTO — 17
ZIZINHO — 17
FERNÁNDEZ, TEODORO — 15
VARELA, SEVERINO — 15
UGARTE, VÍCTOR AGUSTÍN — 11
HORMAZÁBAL, ENRIQUE — 10
IGUARÁN, ARNOLDO — 10
HERNÁNDEZ, LUIS — 9
GONZÁLEZ, AURELIO — 9
VILLALBA, JUAN BAUTISTA — 9
AVILÉS, NEY RAÚL — 6
RAFFO, CARLOS ALBERTO — 6
DOLGETTA, JOSÉ LUIS — 6
WANCHOPE, PAULO — 5
GUEVARA, AMADO — 3
WYNALDA, ERIC — 3
LOPES, WAGNER — 2

WORLD CUP GOALKEEPERS

The Golden Glove Award, introduced in 1994 (and named the Yashin Award until 2010), is awarded to the best goalkeeper of the World Cup finals. Gianluigi Buffon, Iker Casillas, and Manuel Neuer are recent winners in 2006, 2010 and 2014 respectively. At the 2002 FIFA World Cup, German keeper Oliver Kahn became the first and so far only goalkeeper in the tournament's history to win the Golden Ball, the award given to the player voted as the most outstanding at the FIFA World Cup finals.

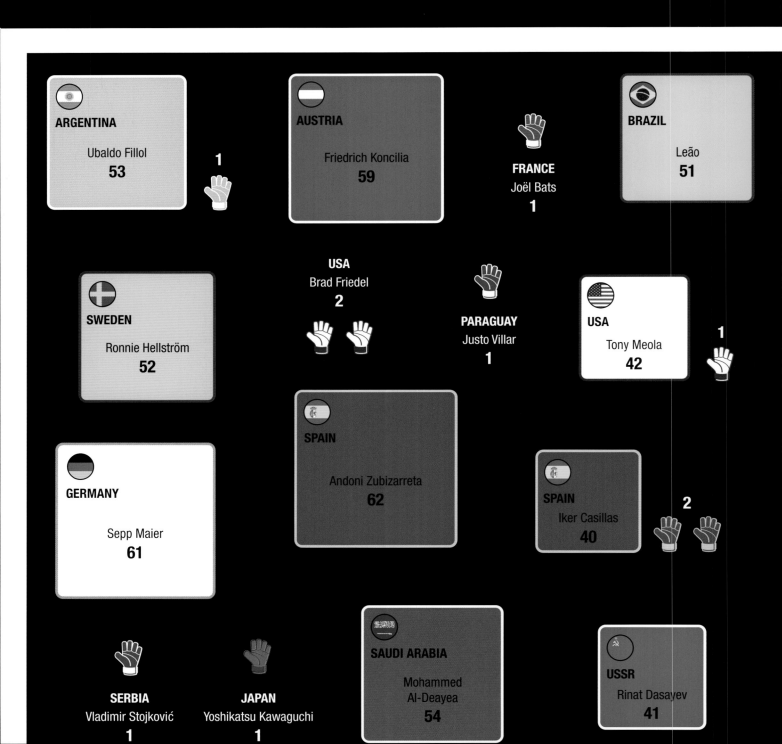

ARGENTINA

Ubaldo Fillol
53

1

AUSTRIA

Friedrich Koncilia
59

FRANCE
Joël Bats
1

BRAZIL

Leão
51

USA
Brad Friedel
2

SWEDEN

Ronnie Hellström
52

PARAGUAY
Justo Villar
1

USA

Tony Meola
42

1

GERMANY

Sepp Maier
61

SPAIN

Andoni Zubizarreta
62

SPAIN

Iker Casillas
40

2

SAUDI ARABIA

Mohammed
Al-Deayea
54

USSR

Rinat Dasayev
41

SERBIA
Vladimir Stojković
1

JAPAN
Yoshikatsu Kawaguchi
1

SAVES

 PENALTY SAVES

Source: Opta (October 2015)
All data from 1966–2014.

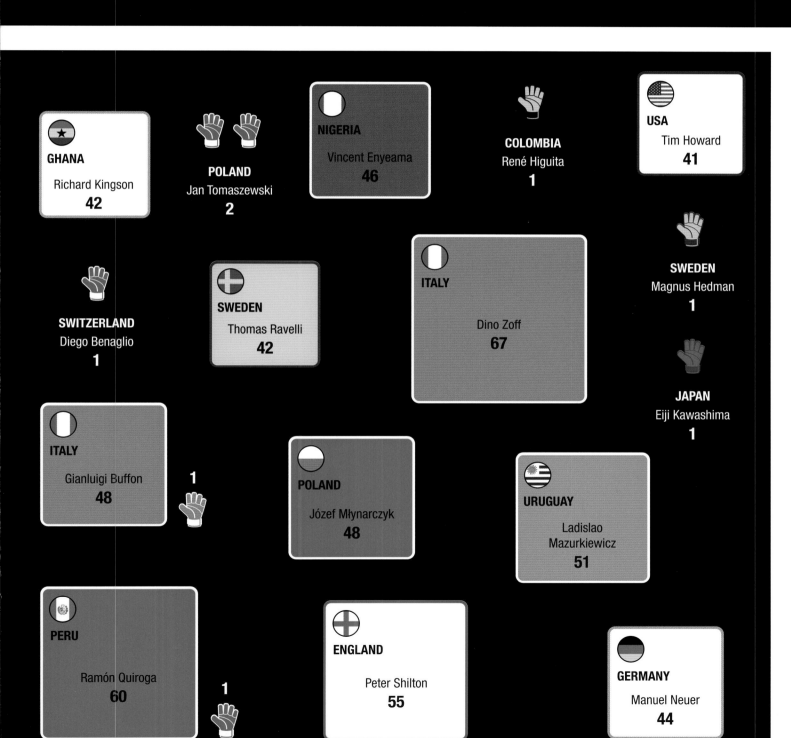

GHANA
Richard Kingson
42

POLAND
Jan Tomaszewski
2

NIGERIA
Vincent Enyeama
46

COLOMBIA
René Higuita
1

USA
Tim Howard
41

SWITZERLAND
Diego Benaglio
1

SWEDEN
Thomas Ravelli
42

ITALY
Dino Zoff
67

SWEDEN
Magnus Hedman
1

JAPAN
Eiji Kawashima
1

ITALY
Gianluigi Buffon
48

1

POLAND
Józef Młynarczyk
48

URUGUAY
Ladislao Mazurkiewicz
51

PERU
Ramón Quiroga
60

1

ENGLAND
Peter Shilton
55

GERMANY
Manuel Neuer
44

BUNDESLIGA GAME WINS

Although there is no doubting the dominance of Bayern München over their Bundesliga rivals, this infographic illustrates the competitive nature of the league. A total of 53 clubs have competed in the Bundesliga over the 30 plus years, with more than 10 teams earning a win ratio of over 40%. Bayern hold the record for the most wins in a season, reaching 29 in both 2012–13 and 2013–14, clocking up a run of 19 games in the latter season. The last two seasons have seen Bayern extend their lead in this category with two emphatic Bundesliga titles, while only Borussia Dortmund, Lokomotive Leipzig and Bayer Leverkusen have recorded better than a 50% win ratio.

Club	Wins
ROT-WEISS ESSEN	61
FC AUGSBURG	64
SV WALDHOF MANNHEIM	71
OFC KICKERS 1901	77
TSG 1899 HOFFENHEIM	103
FC HANSA ROSTOCK	124
1. FSV MAINZ 05	127
KFC UERDINGEN 05	138
DSC ARMINIA BIELEFELD	159
SC FREIBURG	180
TSV 1860 MÜNCHEN	238
KARLSRUHER SC	241
EINTRACHT BRAUNSCHWEIG	242
FORTUNA DÜSSELDORF	245
VFL WOLFSBURG	261
HANNOVER 96	293
MSV DUISBERG	296
1. FC NÜRNBERG	341
VFL BOCHUM 1848	356
HERTHA BSC	421
BAYER 04 LEVERKUSEN	550
1. FC KAISERSLAUTERN	575
EINTRACHT FRANKFURT	592

Under 60 Wins

FC ST PAULI **58**	1. FC SAARBRÜCKEN **32**	STUTTGARTER KICKERS **20**	SC PADERBORN 07 **7**
FC ENERGIE COTTBUS **56**	SV DARMSTADT 98 **28**	RB LEIPZIG **20**	SC PREUSSEN MÜNSTER **7**
ALEMANNIA AACHEN **43**	SC BORUSSIA NEUNKIRCHEN **25**	FC INGOLSTADT **18**	SPVGG GREUTHER FÜRTH **4**
ROT-WEISS OBERHAUSEN **36**	WUPPERTALER SV **25**	TENNIS BORUSSIA BERLIN **11**	BLAU-WEISS 1890 BERLIN **3**
SG WATTENSCHEID 09 **34**	FC 08 HOMBURG **21**	SSV ULM 1846 **9**	VFB LEIPZIG **3**
SG DYNAMO DRESDEN **33**	SPVGG UNTERHACHING **20**	SC FORTUNA KÖLN **8**	TASMANIA 1900 BERLIN **2**

1. FC KÖLN **624**

FC SCHALKE 04 **655**

BORUSSIA MÖNCHENGLADBACH **672**

VFB STUTTGART **718**

HAMBURGER SV **738**

BORUSSIA DORTMUND **746**

SV WERDER BREMEN **761**

BAYERN MÜNCHEN **1043**

1998 WORLD CUP GOALS

Host nation France lit up their own World Cup in 1998, and finished the tournament with the greatest triumph of all – defeating Ronaldo's Brazil in the final. England met Argentina in Saint-Étienne, unarguably the match of the tournament, while five goals secured the Golden Boot for Davor Šuker of Croatia. Rivaldo hit the winner as Brazil and Denmark shared five goals in a riveting quarter-final, while goals such as Michael Owen's run-and-shoot, and Dennis Bergkamp's control-and-finish for the Netherlands – both against Argentina – highlighted that world-class football at its best can transcend any country's border.

DENNIS BERGKAMP – **Netherlands** vs Argentina

Dennis Bergkamp clips it beautifully past Argentinian goalkeeper Carlos Roa, 4 July 1998.

1. Pass (cross, long ball, chipped) **López**
2. Ball recovery **de Boer**
3. Pass (long ball, chipped) **de Boer**
4. Take on **Bergkamp**
5. Challenge **Ayala**
6. Good skill **Bergkamp**
7. Good skill **Bergkamp**
8. Goal **Bergkamp**

KEY

Ball movement	————	Player with ball ············
Shot	———⚽	Player without ball ··············

MICHAEL OWEN – England vs Argentina

1. Take on **López**
2. Tackle **Ince**
3. Ball recovery **Ince**
4. Pass **Ince**
5. Pass **Beckham**
6. Good skill **Owen**
7. Take on **Owen**
8. Challenge **Chamot**
9. Take on **Owen**
10. Goal **Owen**

EMMANUEL PETIT – France vs Brazil

1. Ball recovery
   Dugarry
2. Head pass
   Júnior Baiano
3. Pass **Dugarry**
4. Through ball **Vieira**
5. Goal **Petit**

RONALDO – Brazil vs Morocco

1. Pass (chipped) **Bassir**
2. Head pass **Cafu**
3. Ball recovery **Sampaio**
4. Pass **Sampaio**
5. Launch **Aldair**
6. Head pass **Rossi**
7. Pass **Dunga**
8. Lay-off **Rivaldo**
9. Pass **Dunga**
10. Pass **Bebeto**
11. Through ball (chipped)
    Rivaldo
12. Goal **Ronaldo**

BOUDEWIJN ZENDEN – Netherlands vs Croatia

1. Goal kick (long ball)
   Ladić
2. Head pass **de Boer**
3. Pass **Stanić**
4. Interception **Cocu**
5. Pass **Cocu**
6. Pass **Numan**
7. Pass (long ball) **Jonk**
8. Goal **Zenden**

LONGEST UNBEATEN RUNS

AC Milan

58 Games

Run started on 26 May 1991
0–0 vs Parma FC

Bayern München

53 Games

Run started on 3 November 2012
3–0 vs Hamburger SV

Arsenal

49 Games

Run started on 7 May 2003
6–1 vs Southampton

Real Sociedad

38 Games

Run started on 29 April 1979
1–0 vs Valencia CF

FC Nantes

32 Games

"The Invincibles" was a nickname first given to the 1880s Preston North End team when they won the first "Double", completing the season unbeaten with just four draws. Arsenal would inherit the title in their unbeaten (12-draw) Premier League-winning season of 2003–04. In Europe, Juventus, AC Milan, S.L. Benfica, FC Porto, AFC Ajax and others have all completed an unbeaten campaign, and in 2017, Celtic's now famous "Infrangibles" became the first Scottish team to manage the feat since the nineteenth century. However, no Ligue 1, Bundesliga or modern-era La Liga club have yet run the course of the season without defeat.

Source: Opta (May 2017)

Run ended on 14 March 1993
0–1 vs Parma FC

Run ended on 29 March 2014
0–1 vs FC Augsburg

Run ended on 16 October 2004
0–2 vs Manchester United

Run ended on 4 May 1980
1–2 vs Sevilla FC

Run ended on 8 April 1995
0–2 vs RC Strasbourg Alsace

" It's not impossible [to go through the season unbeaten] as AC Milan once did it but I can't see why it's so shocking to say it. Do you think Manchester United, Liverpool or Chelsea don't dream that as well? They just don't say it because they're scared to look ridiculous, but nobody is ridiculous in this job as we know anything can happen."

Arsène Wenger in 2002, a whole year
before Arsenal's "invincible" season

ASIAN CUP RECORDS BY NATION

The Asian Cup is contested by the nations of the Asian Football Confederation, which stretches from the Middle East to Japan and Australia (who joined the AFC in 2006). It was held every four years from the inaugural 1956 tournament until 2004, then from 2007 (switching to avoid conflicting with the Olympics and European Championship). The number of nations competing in the finals increased from an original four to 12 in 1996, to 16 in 2004 and will increase to 24 in 2019.

QUALIFICATION NOTES
*South Vietnam played in 1956 and 1960, and became one country in 1976.

Australia joined the Asian
Football Confederation in 2006

Winner

Host

Qualified

0	7
1	8
2	9
3	10
4	11
5	12
6	13

DPR Korea

Japan

China

Korea Republic

Chinese Taipei

Hong Kong, China

Vietnam*

Malaysia

Bangladesh

India

Myanmar

Cambodia

Thailand

Indonesia

Singapore

Source: FIFA (October 2015)

117

LA LIGA TOP GOALSCORERS 1998–2017

ROBERTO SOLDADO **110**

GONZALO HIGUAÍN **107**

ANTOINE GRIEZMANN **100**

FERNANDO TORRES **97**

DIEGO TRISTÁN **95**

ROY MAKAAY **93**

RUBÉN CASTRO **92**

ISMAEL URZAIZ **91**

SAVO MILOŠEVIĆ **91**

PATRICK KLUIVERT **90**

FRÉDÉRIC KANOUTÉ **89**

LUIS SUÁREZ **85**

RONALDO **83**

WALTER PANDIANI **82**

FERNANDO MORIENTES **79**

NIHAT KAHVECI **76**

SALVA BALLESTA **75**

SERGIO AGÜERO **74**

LUIS GARCÍA **73**

LUÍS FABIANO **72**

VICTOR **71**

SERGIO GARCÍA **71**

JAVIER SAVIOLA **70**

RONALDINHO **69**

CARLOS VELA **68**

DELY VALDÉS **68**

NEYMAR **68**

DARKO KOVAČEVIĆ **67**

RIVALDO **67**

GIUSEPPE ROSSI **64**

ETXEBERRIA **63**

Lionel Messi, all-time top goalscorer. In November 2012, the prodigious striker began a run of scoring in 21 consecutive games, including a goal against every other La Liga team.

Lionel Messi and Cristiano Ronaldo tower over La Liga goalscoring records. Their lead is considerable, but they also score around a goal a game – almost twice the rate of others in the chart. The only player in the league's history whose record stands the equal of these modern superstars is the great Telma Zarra. He played at Athletic Bilbao for 15 seasons, scoring at nearly a goal a game and helping Bilbao to a league title in 1943. His name now lives on in the award given to La Liga's top goalscorer each season.

In the 2010–11 season Cristiano Ronaldo became the first La Liga player for 20 years to score at a ratio of over a goal per game. Since then the feat has been achieved every season, Lionel Messi achieving the best ratio of 1.44 in 2012–13.

Source: Opta (May 2017)
Stats from La Liga 1998–99 to 2016–17

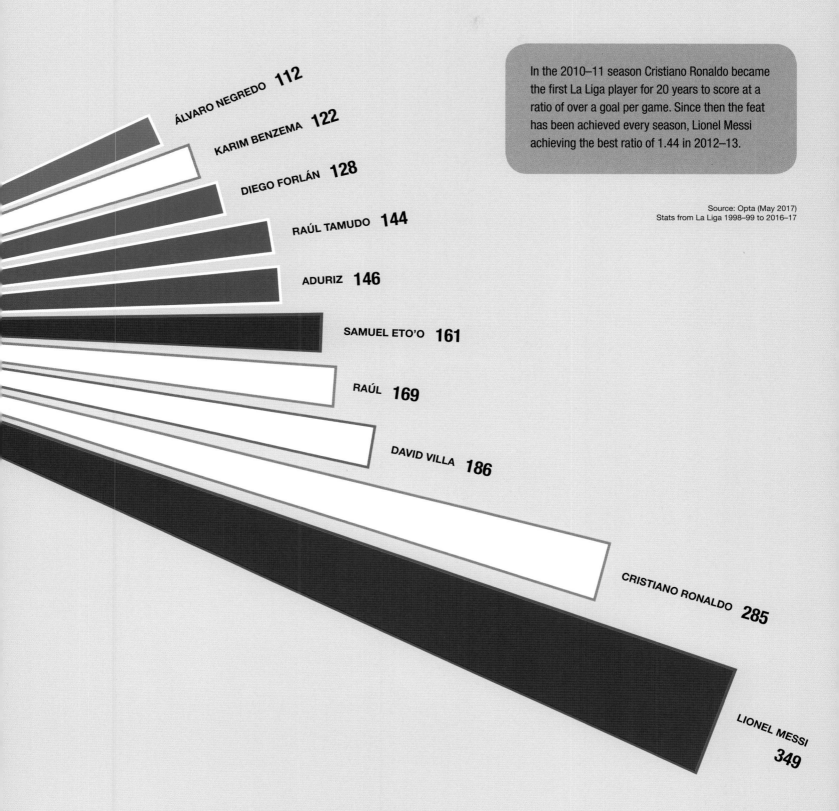

ÁLVARO NEGREDO **112**

KARIM BENZEMA **122**

DIEGO FORLÁN **128**

RAÚL TAMUDO **144**

ADURIZ **146**

SAMUEL ETO'O **161**

RAÚL **169**

DAVID VILLA **186**

CRISTIANO RONALDO **285**

LIONEL MESSI **349**

EUROPEAN CUP WINS BY NATION

The recent Champions League successes of Barcelona and Real Madrid have secured Spain's claim to be most successful European nation. Real Madrid's consecutive triumphs in the European Cup's first five competitions help Spain top the list, although England have had more successful clubs and Italy have had more finalists. In later years, the concentration of financial might in Europe's major leagues has increased the dominance of those nations. The era of the Champions League (beginning in 1992) has seen Spain register 10 wins, followed by Italy (five), England (four) and Germany (three).

Internazionale Milano — 3

Juventus — 2

Steaua București — 1

Marseille — 1

1 France

1 Romania

12 Italy

12 Real Madrid

7 AC Milan

Feyenoord — 1

PSV Eindhoven — 1

6 The Netherlands

4 Ajax

17 Spain

Barcelona — 5

1 Chelsea
1 Aston Viilla
Nottingham Forest
2
12 England
3 Manchester United
5 Liverpool

1 Borussia Dortmund
Hamburger SV
1
7 Germany
5 Bayern München

1 Celtic
1 Scotland

Porto 2
4 Portugal
1 Red Star Belgrade
2 Benfica
1 Yugoslavia

Source: Opta (June 2017)

FOOTBALL RIVALRIES: PART 3

Football fans know that it's the tough and tense matches between fierce rivals that really heighten their emotions during a season. AFC Ajax vs Feyenoord, for example, has become the most ferocious game in the Netherlands as the capital's city slickers do battle with the working-class port labourers. In Turkey's capital Istanbul, neighbours Fenerbahçe S.K. and Galatasaray S.K. continue a rivalry more than 100 years old. Across the Atlantic Ocean, it is New York City FC and the New York Red Bulls that have developed a more recent mutual antagonism after just a handful of matches.

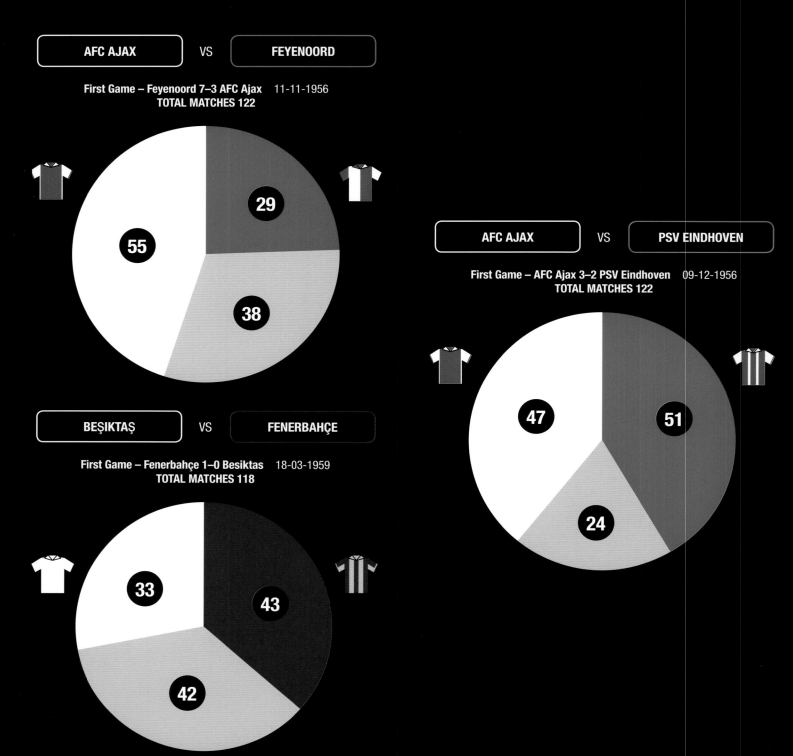

| AFC AJAX | VS | FEYENOORD |

First Game – Feyenoord 7–3 AFC Ajax   11-11-1956
TOTAL MATCHES 122

55   29   38

| AFC AJAX | VS | PSV EINDHOVEN |

First Game – AFC Ajax 3–2 PSV Eindhoven   09-12-1956
TOTAL MATCHES 122

47   51   24

| BEŞIKTAŞ | VS | FENERBAHÇE |

First Game – Fenerbahçe 1–0 Besiktas   18-03-1959
TOTAL MATCHES 118

33   43   42

It's nowhere near as steeped in history as El Clasico or the Old Firm Derby, but New York is growing its own bitterly fought rivalry. The Hudson River Derby pitches the New York Red Bulls who play in New Jersey against their neighbours NYCFC, who set up home in Yankee Stadium in the Bronx. New York Red Bulls had been established for nearly 20 years (with sworn enemies in Washington's DC United) before neighbours NYCFC arrived in 2015. They dealt out four beatings before the newcomers finally tasted victory.

FENERBAHÇE vs GALATASARAY

First Game – Fenerbahçe 1–0 Galatasaray   17-12-1959
TOTAL MATCHES 120

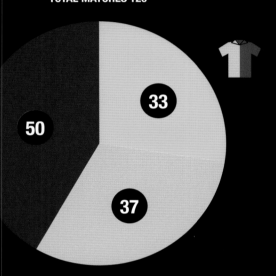

BEŞİKTAŞ vs GALATASARAY

First Game – Besiktas 1–0 Galatasaray   02-12-1959
TOTAL MATCHES 118

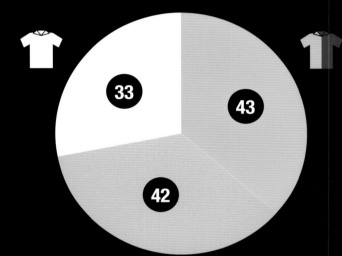

LA GALAXY vs SAN JOSE EARTHQUAKES

First Game – LA Galaxy 2–0 San Jose Earthquakes   03-04-2008
TOTAL MATCHES 27

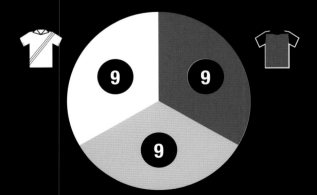

NEW YORK CITY FC vs NEW YORK RED BULLS

First Game – New York Red Bulls 2–1 New York City FC   10-05-2015
TOTAL MATCHES 6

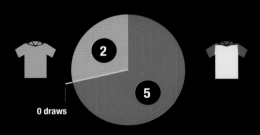

0 draws

Source: Opta (May 2017)

SERIE A GAME WINS

There are 65 teams who have participated in the 84 Serie A championships to have taken place to date, with only Internazionale having competed in every season. Apart from the largely pre-war success of Torino and Bologna, Serie A has been dominated by *Le Sette Sorelle* (The Seven Sisters): Juventus, Roma, Milan, Inter, Fiorentina, Lazio – and Parma, who have more recently been replaced by Napoli. The Italian league is usually secured by a team amassing a total of around 25 victories in the season, although Juventus won 33 and 29 out of 38 respectively in their title-winning seasons of 2013–14 and 2015–16.

EMPOLI **108**
COMO **109**
ASCOLI **110**
LECCE **114**
PRO PATRIA **118**
PERUGIA **126**
MODENA **130**
NOVARA **133**
ALESSANDRIA **136**
SPAL **151**
CATANIA **162**
LIVORNO **171**
CHIEVO **174**
PADOVA **182**
BRESCIA **188**
VERONA **227**
TRIESTINA **253**
BARI **258**
VICENZA **296**
PALERMO **307**
PARMA **327**
CAGLIARI **371**
UDINESE **498**
GENOA **543**
ATALANTA **554**
SAMPDORIA **682**
BOLOGNA **840**
TORINO **884**

Under 100 Wins

FOGGIA **95**	PRO VERCELLI **65**	PESCARA **36**	CARPI **9**
VENEZIA **94**	SASSUOLO **50**	VARESE **36**	CROTONE **9**
REGGINA **83**	MANTOVA **48**	CASALE **33**	ANCONA **8**
SIENA **83**	LIGURIA **44**	SAMPIERDARENESE **24**	FROSINONE **8**
CESENA **80**	CREMONESE **43**	SALERNITANA **23**	TERNANA **7**
LUCCHESE **80**	PISA **42**	LECCO **19**	PISTOIESE **6**
AVELLINO **79**	MESSINA **39**	LEGNANO **16**	TREVISO **3**
PIACENZA **65**	CATANZARO **38**	REGGIANA **16**	

NAPOLI **911**

LAZIO **935**

FIORENTINA **1054**

ROMA **1170**

AC MILAN **1340**

INTERNAZIONALE MILANO **1404**

JUVENTUS **1525**

2002 WORLD CUP GOALS

Japan and South Korea co-hosted Asia's first World Cup in 2002 and it is a tournament remembered for being full of surprises. Reigning champions France and fancied favourites Argentina went home after the group stage and South Korea beat Spain, Italy and Portugal on their way to the semi-finals. Few fans were shocked, however, by Brazil's clear run to victory, powered by a player at the top of his game – Ronaldo. The chest and volley by Uruguay's Diego Forlán, Matt Holland's superstrike for Ireland and the overhead kick by Brazil's Edmílson are goals also still regularly voted in World Cup Greatest Goals lists, along with these ones too...

JARED BORGETTI – Mexico vs Italy

Mexico's Jared Borgetti scored the first goal against Italy with a knockout strike past goalkeeper Gianluigi Buffon, 13 June 2002.

1. Clearance **Vidrio**
2. Tackle **Carmona**
3. Take on **Inzaghi**
4. Ball recovery **Torrado**
5. Pass **Torrado**
6. Pass **Márquez**
7. Pass **Luna**
8. Pass **Márquez**
9. Pass **Carmona**
10. Pass **Rodríguez**
11. Pass **Blanco**
12. Pass **Arellano**
13. Pass **Blanco**
14. Pass **Torrado**
15. Pass **Vidrio**
16. Pass (long ball) **Torrado**
17. Pass **Morales**
18. Pass **Luna**
19. Pass (chipped) **Blanco**
20. Goal **Borgetti**

KEY

Ball movement	▬▬▬▬	Player with ball	··············
Shot	▬▬▬◆	Player without ball	··············

SALIF DIAO – Senegal vs Denmark

1. Take on **Jørgenson**
2. Tackle **Camara**
3. Ball recovery **Camara**
4. Pass **Camara**
5. Pass **Diouf**
6. Pass (long ball) **Diao**
7. Through ball **Fadiga**
8. Goal **Diao**

EDMÍLSON – Brazil vs Costa Rica

1. Pass **Wanchope**
2. Interception **Silva**
3. Pass **Cafu**
4. Ball recovery **Cafu**
5. Pass **Cafu**
6. Pass **Juninho**
7. Pass **Cafu**
8. Pass **Edmílson**
9. Pass **Silva**
10. Pass **Edmílson**
11. Pass **Rivaldo**
12. Pass **Edmílson**
13. Pass (cross, chipped) **Júnior**
14. Goal **Edmílson**

RONALDINHO – Brazil vs England

1. Goal (free kick) **Ronaldinho**

CHRISTIAN VIERI – Italy vs Ecuador

1. Throw in **Panucci**
2. Pass **Totti**
3. Head pass **Di Biagio**
4. Pass **Tommasi**
5. Through ball **Totti**
6. Attempt saved **Vieri**
7. Save (parried danger) **Cevallos**
8. Clearance **Hurtado**
9. Head pass **Cannavaro**
10. Pass (long ball, chipped) **Tommasi**
11. Pass (long ball, chipped) **Panucci**
12. Pull back **Totti**
13. Goal **Vieri**

Source: Opta (October 2015)

MLS TROPHY WINS PER CLUB

Major League Soccer (MLS), the top tier of football in USA and Canada, was inspired by the success of the 1994 World Cup in the USA. The league's first season took place in 1996 and consisted of ten teams. In the following 20 years the number of teams has expanded to 22 – including three teams from Canada – with further expansion planned for 2020. Organized into an Eastern and Western conference, clubs compete for a place in the national play-offs to represent their conference in a final to win the MLS – also known as the Philip F. Anschutz Trophy.

Source: Opta (October 2016)

Key (from top)

- LA GALAXY **5**
- D.C. UNITED **4**
- SAN JOSE EARTHQUAKES **2**
- HOUSTON DYNAMO **2**
- SPORTING KANSAS CITY **2**
- CHICAGO FIRE **1**
- COLUMBUS CREW **1**
- REAL SALT LAKE **1**
- COLORADO RAPIDS **1**
- PORTLAND TIMBERS **1**
- SEATTLE SOUNDERS **1**

LA GALAXY **5**

D.C. UNITED **4**

SAN JOSE EARTHQUAKES,
HOUSTON DYNAMO,
SPORTING KANSAS CITY **2**

CHICAGO FIRE,
COLUMBUS CREW,
REAL SALT LAKE,
COLORADO RAPIDS,
PORTLAND TIMBERS,
SEATTLE SOUNDERS **1**

2007 2008 2009 2010 2011 2012 2013 2014 2015 2016

WORLD CUP GOALSCORERS BY COUNTRY

It was Lucien Laurent, for France, who scored the first World Cup finals goal at the 1930 competition. Since then over 2,300 goals have been scored by 80 different countries in 20 finals tournaments. Germany and Brazil have both been tournament top scorers on four occasions,

GERMANY

Miroslav Klose
16

Jürgen Klinsmann
11

Thomas Müller
10

Helmut Rahn
10

Uwe Seeler
9

Rudi Völler
8

Max Morlock
6

Helmut Haller
6

Gerd Müller
14

Karl-Heinz Rummenigge
9

Hans Schäfer
7

Lothar Matthäus
6

Lukas Podolski
5

Franz Beckenbauer
5

ITALY

Roberto Baggio
9

Paolo Rossi
9

Salvatore Schillaci
6

Christian Vieri
9

Alessandro Altobelli
5

Silvio Piola
5

ARGENTINA

Gabriel Batistuta
10

Diego Maradona
8

Mario Alberto Kempes
6

Guillermo Stábile
8

Lionel Messi
5

Gonzalo Higuaín
5

BRAZIL

Ronaldo
15

Vavá
9

Rivaldo
8

Ademir
8

Jairzinho
9

Careca
7

Bebeto
6

Garrincha
5

Pelé
12

Leônidas da Silva
8

Rivellino
6

Zico
5

Romário
5

NETHERLANDS

Johnny Rep
7

Wesley Sneijder
6

Robin van Persie
6

Dennis Bergkamp
6

Arjen Robben
6

Rob Rensenbrink
6

Johan Neeskens
5

Hungary have the highest strike rate at 2.72 goals scored per match (helped by their record 27 goals in 1954), while Canada, China, Dutch East Indies, Trinidad and Tobago, and Zaire all have reached the finals but failed to register a single goal – a notable achievement in itself.

Source: Opta (August 2015)

SPAIN

David Villa **9**

Fernando Morientes **5**

Fernando Hierro **5**

Emilio Butragueño **5**

Raúl **5**

Basora **5**

FRANCE

Just Fontaine **13**

Thierry Henry **6**

Michel Platini **5**

Zinedine Zidane **5**

HUNGARY

Sándor Kocsis **11**

Lajos Tichy **7**

György Sárosi **6**

Gyula Zsengellér **5**

URUGUAY

Óscar Míguez **8**

Diego Forlán **6**

Juan Alberto Schiaffino **5**

Luis Suárez **5**

Pedro Cea **5**

ENGLAND

Gary Lineker **10**

Geoff Hurst **5**

CZECHOSLOVAKIA

Oldřich Nejedlý **7**

Tomáš Skuhravý **5**

AUSTRIA

Erich Probst **6**

Hans Krankl **5**

PERU

Teófilo Cubillas **10**

SWEDEN

Henrik Larsson **5**

Kennet Andersson **5**

BULGARIA

Hristo Stoichkov **6**

GHANA

Asamoah Gyan **6**

RUSSIA

Oleg Salenko **6**

COLOMBIA

James Rodríguez **6**

AUSTRALIA

Tim Cahill **5**

CROATIA

Davor Šuker **6**

BELGIUM

Marc Wilmots **5**

CAMEROON

Roger Milla **5**

POLAND

Grzegorz Lato **10**

Andrzej Szarmach **7**

Zbigniew Boniek **6**

PORTUGAL

Eusébio **9**

SWITZERLAND

Josef Hügi **6**

DENMARK

Jon Dahl Tomasson **5**

NORTHERN IRELAND

Peter McParland **5**

USA

Landon Donovan **5**

USSR

Valentin Ivanov **5**

GOALS PER GAME PER DECADE

Watch any major European match this year and you can expect to see around 2.5 goals. The goals-per-game ratio has declined steadily from four per match in the late 1950s to its current level, but has shown signs of rising again in the era of Messi, Cavani and Aubameyang. You'll need to head to Puerto Rico, Taiwan or Bermuda to have a good chance of a four goal top-flight match, while games in Tanzania, Lesotho and Jordan struggle to register two.

German Bundesliga not formed until 1965.

"If you want to have fun, you should go to the circus." With these words Juventus coach Massimiliano Allegri defended his club's safety-first approach. Italian teams' reputation for defensive football is borne out in the tables below as *Catenaccio* and defensive prowess took hold from the 1950s. But there are signs of change – in 2016/17 there were 2.88 goals per game in the league, the highest since 1951, backing up claims of a transformation of Serie A football into an often end-to-end entertaining spectacle.

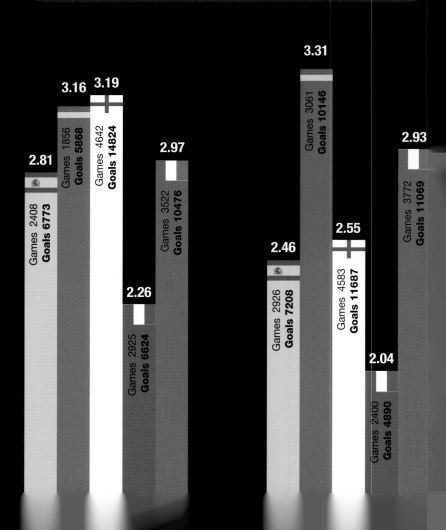

AVERAGE GOALS PER GAME

4.0

3.5

3.0

2.5

2.0

0

3.69 — Games 2357 Goals 8695
3.38 — Games 4608 Goals 15585
2.84 — Games 3228 Goals 9181
3.32 — Games 3210 Goals 10655
0*
2.81 — Games 2408 Goals 6773
3.16 — Games 1856 Goals 5868
3.19 — Games 4642 Goals 14824
2.26 — Games 2925 Goals 6624
2.97 — Games 3522 Goals 10476
2.46 — Games 2926 Goals 7208
3.31 — Games 3061 Goals 10146
2.55 — Games 4583 Goals 11687
2.04 — Games 2400 Goals 4890
2.93 — Games 3772 Goals 11069

...rt Lewandowski, the ...undesliga's greatest ...dern-day goalscorer. ...he Polish striker has ...ed 151 league goals ... Borussia Dortmund ...nd Bayern München since 2010.

Source: Opta (May 2017)

3.29 — Games 3095 · Goals **10173**

...7 — Goals **8246**

2.65 — Games 4448 · Goals **11771**

2.09 — Games 2506 · Goals **5230**

2.49 — Games 3819 · Goals **9497**

2.57 — Games 3964 · Goals **10189**

2.84 — Games 3099 · Goals **8792**

2.61 — Games 4122 · Goals **10770**

2.55 — Games 3034 · Goals **7723**

2.30 — Games 3601 · Goals **8270**

2.64 — Games 3780 · Goals **9984**

2.77 — Games 3060 · Goals **8470**

2.60 — Games 3801 · Goals **9886**

2.60 — Games 3470 · Goals **9007**

2.29 — Games 3587 · Goals **8216**

2.77 — Games 2890 · Goals **8014**

2.91 — Games 2295 · Goals **6667**

2.74 — Games 2844 · Goals **7790**

2.67 — Games 2873 · Goals **7659**

2.49 — Games 2851 · Goals **7095**

LA LIGA GAME WINS PER CLUB

According to UEFA, La Liga has been the top league in Europe since 2012, and it has produced the continent's top-rated club twice as often as any other league. Few will be surprised to find the La Liga giants Real Madrid and Barcelona dominating this most wins chart, but may be astounded by just how evenly matched they are. Even Real Madrid's 2011–12 record of 32 wins in a season was matched by Barcelona the following season and, although it took them until 2016, Real Madrid eventually equalled Barcelona's 2010–11 record of 16 consecutive victories.

ELCHE **20**
TENERIFE **26**
REAL OVIEDO **33**
EIBAR **35**
NUMANCIA **37**
RECREATIVO **42**
LAS PALMAS **44**
GRANADA CF **56**
SPORTING DE GIJÓN **61**
ALMERÍA **62**
ALAVÉS **90**
LEVANTE **95**
RAYO VALLECANO **111**
REAL VALLADOLID **120**
RACING DE SANTANDER **141**
GETAFE **147**
REAL ZARAGOZA **156**
OSASUNA **172**
REAL BETIS **178**
CELTA DE VIGO **187**
MÁLAGA **204**
MALLORCA **210**
REAL SOCIEDAD **217**
ESPANYOL **242**

> **"You want to win games, break records but I don't do it just for the records. I do it because I want to improve and see my players improve."**
>
> Zinedine Zidane, Real Madrid coach

Under 20 Wins

ALBACETE	19	LEGANÉS	8
REAL MURCIA	12	XEREZ	8
HÉRCULES	9	SALAMANCA	7
CF EXTREMADURA	9	GIMNÀSTIC DE TARRAGON	7
CÁDIZ	8	CÓRDOBA	3

DEPORTIVO DE LA CORUÑA **247**

VILLARREAL **266**

ATHLETIC BILBAO **273**

SEVILLA **285**

ATLÉTICO MADRID **300**

VALENCIA CF **339**

BARCELONA **467**

REAL MADRID **475**

FOOTBALL STADIUMS BY SIZE

The footballing world may still mourn the loss of iconic grounds such as Arsenal's Highbury stadium, Benfica's Estádio da Luz and Athletic Bilbao's La Catedral at San Mamés, but the stadiums that replaced them and other new venues such as the Allianz Arena in Munich, Juventus' stadium in Turin and Atlético Madrid's Wanda Metropolitano look set to join Camp Nou, Old Trafford and La Bombonera on the list of the world's most hallowed grounds. This infographic illustrates the world's biggest football stadiums (on this page) and the homes of leading football clubs and major national teams (facing) – and, for comparison, includes two of the smallest.

Source: Google (May 2017)

RUNGRADO MAY DAY STADIUM
Pyongyang, North Korea

DPR KOREA NATIONAL FOOTBALL TEAM
150,000

CAMP NOU
Barcelona, Spain

BARCELONA
99,354

FNB STADIUM (SOCCER CITY)
Johannesburg, South Africa

**SOUTH AFRICA NATIONAL TEAM,
KAIZER CHIEFS, 2010 WORLD CUP**
94,736

WEMBLEY STADIUM
London, England

**ENGLAND NATIONAL
FOOTBALL TEAM**
90,000

ESTADIO AZTECA
Mexico City, Mexico

**MEXICO NATIONAL FOOTBALL TEAM,
CLUB AMÉRICA**
87,000

BORG EL ARAB STADIUM
Alexandria, Egypt

**EGYPT NATIONAL
FOOTBALL TEAM**
86,000

SALT LAKE STADIUM
Kolkata, India

**INDIA NATIONAL
FOOTBALL TEAM**
85,000

SIGNAL IDUNA PARK (WESTFALENSTADION)
Dortmund, Germany
BORUSSIA DORTMUND
81,359

STADE DE FRANCE
Saint-Denis, France
FRANCE NATIONAL FOOTBALL TEAM
81,338

SANTIAGO BERNABÉU STADIUM
Madrid, Spain
REAL MADRID
81,044

LUZHNIKI STADIUM
Moscow, Russia
**RUSSIA NATIONAL FOOTBALL TEAM,
2018 WORLD CUP FINAL**
81,000

STADIO GIUSEPPE MEAZZA (SAN SIRO)
Milan, Italy
INTERNAZIONALE MILANO, AC MILAN
80,018

MARACANÃ STADIUM
Rio De Janeiro, Brazil
**BRAZIL NATIONAL TEAM,
CR FLAMENGO, FLUMINENSE FC,
BOTAFOGO FR**
78,383

OLD TRAFFORD
Manchester, England
MANCHESTER UNITED F.C.
75,643

ALLIANZ ARENA
Munich, Germany
**BAYERN MÜNCHEN,
TSV 1860 MUNICH**
75,024

PRINCIPALITY (MILLENNIUM) STADIUM
Cardiff, Wales
WALES NATIONAL FOOTBALL TEAM
74,500

STADIO OLIMPICO
Rome, Italy
A.S. ROMA, S.S. LAZIO
72,630

OLYMPIC STADIUM ATHENS (SPIROS LOUIS)
Athens, Greece
**GREECE NATIONAL FOOTBALL TEAM,
AEK ATHENS, PANATHINAIKOS FC**
69,618

ESTÁDIO DA LUZ
Lisbon, Portugal
**S.L. BENFICA, UEFA EURO 2004 FINAL,
2014 UEFA CHAMPIONS LEAGUE FINAL**
65,647

CELTIC PARK
Glasgow, Scotland
CELTIC FC
60,832

EMIRATES STADIUM
London, England
ARSENAL
60,432

AMSTERDAM ARENA
Amsterdam, Netherlands
**AJAX, NETHERLANDS NATIONAL
FOOTBALL TEAM**
54,033

STADE LOUIS II
Monaco
AS MONACO
18,500

VICTORIA STADIUM
Gibraltar
GIBRALTAR NATIONAL TEAM
5,000

ESTADI COMUNAL D'ANDORRA LA VELLA
La Vella, Andorra
ANDORRA NATIONAL TEAM
1,300

2006 WORLD CUP GOALS

The 2006 World Cup, hosted by Germany, will forever be dominated by one image: the world's greatest footballer, Zinedine Zidane, playing his last game ever, headbutting Italy's Marco Materazzi in the chest. In a low-scoring tournament, five goals were enough to reward Germany's Miroslav Klose the Golden Boot, while Philipp Lahm's wonderstrike in the opening game, Bakari Koné's solo effort for the Ivory Coast and Argentina's Cambiasso finishing an exquisite 24-pass movement stood out as the tournament's best goals.

ESTEBAN CAMBIASSO – Argentina vs Serbia & Montenegro

Esteban Cambiasso celebrates in style after scoring the second goal against Serbia & Montenegro, 16 June 2006.

1. Dispossesed **Kežman**
2. Challenge **Mascherano**
3. Tackle **Rodríguez**
4. Ball recovery **Heinze**
5. Pass **Heinze**
6. Pass **Mascherano**
7. Pass **Riquelme**
8. Pass **Rodríguez**
9. Pass **Sorín**
10. Pass **Rodríguez**
11. Pass **Sorín**
12. Pass **Mascherano**
13. Pass **Riquelme**
14. Pass **Ayala**
15. Pass **Cambiasso**
16. Pass **Mascherano**
17. Pass **Rodríguez**
18. Pass **Sorín**
19. Pass **Rodríguez**
20. Pass **Cambiasso**
21. Pass **Riquelme**
22. Pass **Mascherano**
23. Pass **Mascherano**
24. Pass **Saviola**
25. Pass **Riquelme**
26. Pass **Saviola**
27. Pass **Cambiasso**
28. Pass **Crespo**
29. Goal **Cambiasso**

KEY

Ball movement	Player with ball
Shot	Player without ball

JOE COLE – England vs Sweden

1. Clearance **Alexandersson**
2. Good skill **Cole**
3. Goal **Cole**

DECO – Portugal vs Iran

1. Launch **Nosrati**
2. Head pass **Meira**
3. Head pass **Maniche**
4. Ball recovery **Carvalho**
5. Pass **Carvalho**
6. Pass **Maniche**
7. Pass **Ronaldo**
8. Pass (long ball) **Deco**
9. Pass **Figo**
10. Goal **Deco**

MAXI RODRÍGUEZ – Argentina vs Mexico

1. Pass **Pineda**
2. Pass **Ayala**
3. Pass **Aimar**
4. Pass **Scaloni**
5. Pass **Messi**
6. Pass **Riquelme**
7. Pass (long ball) **Messi**
8. Pass (chipped, long ball) **Sorín**
9. Goal **Rodríguez**

FERNANDO TORRES – Spain vs Ukraine

1. Pass **Shelayev**
2. Interception **Puyol**
3. Take on **Puyol**
4. Pass **Puyol**
5. Challenge **Tymoshchuk**
6. Pass **Torres**
7. Pass **Fàbregas**
8. Flick-on **Puyol**
9. Goal **Torres**

Source: Opta (October 2015)

EREDIVISIE GOALS PER CLUB

Of course, the "big three" Netherlands' teams dominate the goal-scoring tables – Ajax even managed 122 in one season in 1966–67 and PSV's Coen Dillen, nicknamed "Het Kanon", struck 43 times in 1956–57. The modern Dutch goal masters – Cruyff, van Basten, Bergkamp, Van Nistelrooy – all figure as season's top scorers, but the lesser known Ruud Geels was the leading striker on five occasions (four times for Ajax, once for Sparta) between 1974 and 1981. More recently the minor teams strikers have topped the charts on several occasions, including Wilfrid Bony for Vitesse (2012–13), Alfreð Finnbogason of Heerenveen (2013–14) and AZ's Vincent Janssen (2015–16).

> **"Players today can only shoot with their laces. I could shoot with the inside, laces, and outside of both feet. In other words, I was six times better than today's players."**
>
> Johan Cruyff

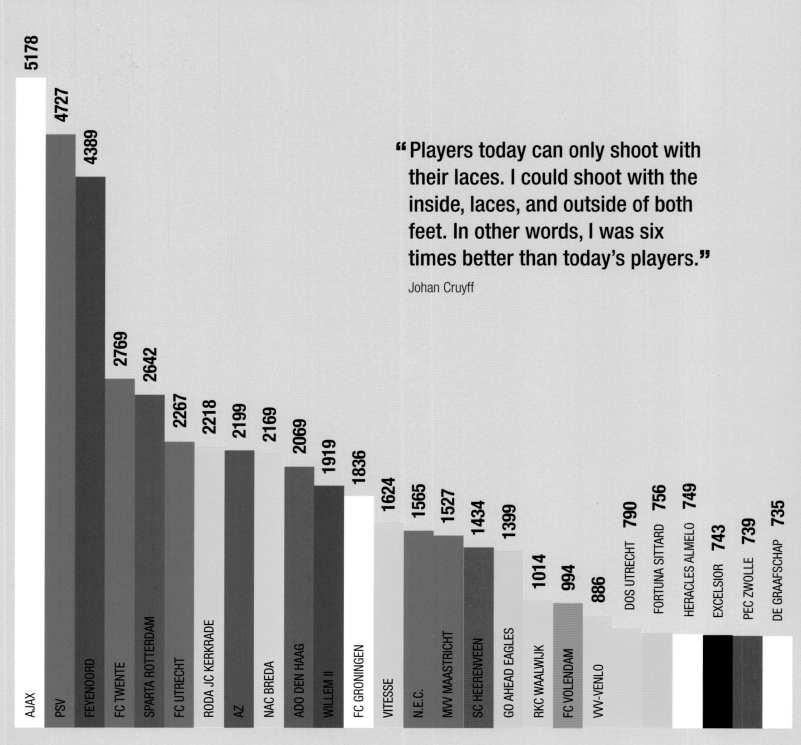

Club	Goals
AJAX	5178
PSV	4727
FEYENOORD	4389
FC TWENTE	2769
SPARTA ROTTERDAM	2642
FC UTRECHT	2267
RODA JC KERKRADE	2218
AZ	2199
NAC BREDA	2169
ADO DEN HAAG	2069
WILLEM II	1919
FC GRONINGEN	1836
VITESSE	1624
N.E.C.	1565
MVV MAASTRICHT	1527
SC HEERENVEEN	1434
GO AHEAD EAGLES	1399
RKC WAALWIJK	1014
FC VOLENDAM	994
VVV-VENLO	886
DOS UTRECHT	790
FORTUNA SITTARD	756
HERACLES ALMELO	749
EXCELSIOR	743
PEC ZWOLLE	739
DE GRAAFSCHAP	735

WILLY VAN DER KUIJLEN	311	RUUD GEELS	265	JOHAN CRUYFF	215	KEES KIST	212
TONNY VAN DER LINDEN	206	HENK GROOT	195	PETER HOUTMAN	180	SJAAK SWART	175
LEO VAN VEEN	174	COR VAN DER GIJP	162	WIM KIEFT	158	DIRK KUYT	153
HALLVAR THORESEN	152	HENK "CHARLY" BOSVELD	152	JOHN BOSMAN	146	PIET KEIZER	146
LEX SCHOENMAKER	145	WILLY BROKAMP	145	JAN VENNEGOOR OF HESSELINK	134	CEES VAN KOOTEN	134
PIET KRUIVER	133	OVE KINDVALL	129	MARTIN VAN GEEL	127	MARCO VAN BASTEN	127
RONALD KOEMAN	126	PIET KEUR	126	THEO DE JONG	126	WILLEM VAN HANEGEM	126
PIERRE VAN HOOIJDONK	125	GERALD VANENBURG	124	COEN DILLEN	120	KLAAS NUNINGA	120
DICK NANNINGA	118	RENÉ VAN DE KERKHOF	118	MATTHEW AMOAH	116	BLAISE NKUFO	114
LEO CANJELS	114	HENK WERY	113	JON DAHL TOMASSON	112	HENNIE MEIJER	111
LUC NILIS	110	KLAAS-JAN HUNTELAAR	109	JACQUES VISSCHERS	109	DICK VAN DIJK	109
ANDRÉ HOEKSTRA	106	MATEJA KEŽMAN	105	CHRIS COENEN	105	KENNETH PEREZ	105
JOHN VAN LOEN	104	CAROL SCHUURMAN	104				

Source: Opta (May 2017)
Colour relates to the team for which the player scored the highest number of goals.

Team	Goals
HAARLEM	695
FORTUNA '54 GELEEN	635
DWS	588
SC ENSCHEDE	565
GVAV	533
TELSTAR	530
FC DEN BOSCH	491
BLAUW-WIT	334
RAPID JC HEERLEN	307
ELINKWIJK	306
FC AMSTERDAM	263
SC CAMBUUR	258
FC DORDRECHT	208
NOAD	187
SHS	168
RBC ROOSENDAAL	164
SITTARDIA	148
BVV	126
FC EINDHOVEN	107
BVC AMSTERDAM	103
DE VOLEWIJCKERS	99
HELMOND SPORT	93
XERXESDZB	92
VEENDAM	74
WAGENINGEN	72
SVV	62
ALKMAAR	39

COPA LIBERTADORES WINS BY NATION

Copa Libertadores de América is the most prestigious club tournament in South America. It is broadcast in over 130 countries and watched by more than a billion viewers. Played annually from February through qualifying, group stages and then a home and away knock-out stage, the tournament is now contested by 38 teams from eleven countries (including Mexican teams since 2000). At least three clubs from each country compete in the tournament with Argentina and Brazil each entitled to enter five teams.

The 2016 final between Colombia's Atletico Nacional and Independiente del Valle of Ecuador was the first between teams from countries on South America's Pacific coast and also the first in 25 years not to feature Argentinian or Brazilian sides.

- ① Atlético Mineiro
- ③ São Paolo
- ① Corinthians
- ① Vasco da Gama
- ③ Santos
- ① Flamengo
- ① Palmeiras
- **17** Brazil
- ② Internacional
- ② Grêmio
- ② Cruzeiro
- ① Colo-Colo
- **1** Chile
- ③ Nacional
- ⑤ Peñarol
- **8** Uruguay

① Once Caldas

② Atlético Nacional

3
Colombia

LDU Quito
①
1
Ecuador

Racing Club de Avellaneda ①

San Lorenzo ①

Vélez Sársfield ①

Argentinos Juniors ①

Independiente ⑦

④ Estudiantes

24
Argentina

③ River Plate

Boca Juniors ⑥

Olimpia
③
3
Paraguay

Source: Opta (July 2016)

LIGUE 1 TITLE WINNERS

Ligue 1 has been graced by 69 teams in its history, with a third of them making a serious impression on league records. The sixth-ranked league in Europe, it has seen one of the most evident shifts between traditional clubs and those benefitting from wealthy benefactors and investors. Those familiar with the recent success of PSG might find it surprising to view their win record still lagging some way behind the league's long-standing clubs, including Sochaux, now a Ligue 2 side and still living off their glories of the 1930s and 1960s.

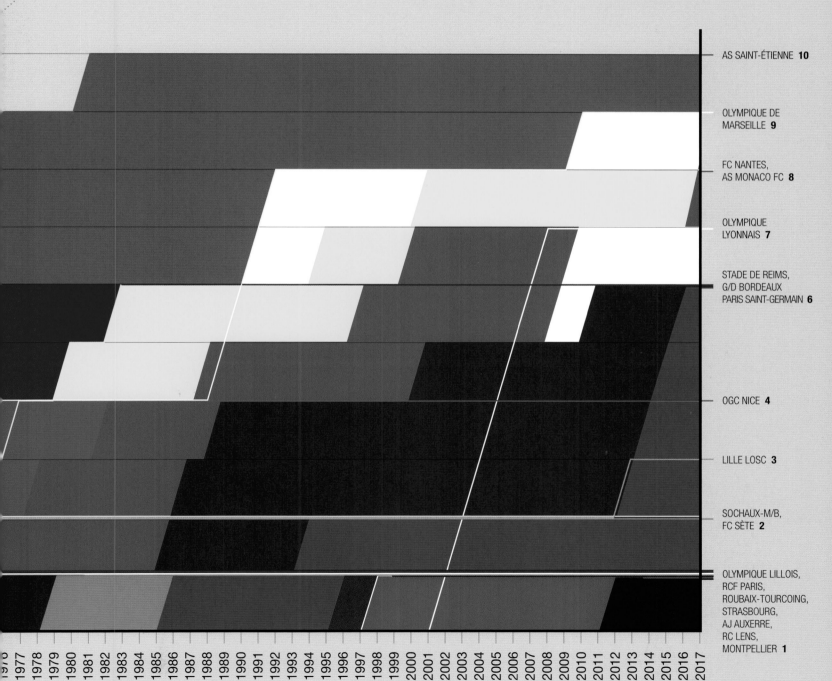

Key (anticlockwise from top-right)

- AS SAINT-ÉTIENNE **10**
- OLYMPIQUE DE MARSEILLE **9**
- FC NANTES **8**
- AS MONACO FC **8**
- OLYMPIQUE LYONNAIS **7**
- GIRONDINS DE BORDEAUX **6**
- STADE DE REIMS **6**

- PARIS SAINT-GERMAIN **6**
- OGC NICE **4**
- LILLE LOSC **3**
- FC SÈTE 34 **2**
- FC SOCHAUX-MONTBÉLIARD **2**
- AJ AUXERRE **1**

- OLYMPIQUE LILLOIS **1**
- MONTPELLIER HÉRRAULT SC **1**
- RC LENS **1**
- RCF PARIS **1**
- CO ROUBAIX-TOURCOING **1**
- RC STRASBOURG ALSACE **1**

Source: Opta (May 2017)

AS SAINT-ÉTIENNE **10**

OLYMPIQUE DE MARSEILLE **9**

FC NANTES, AS MONACO FC **8**

OLYMPIQUE LYONNAIS **7**

STADE DE REIMS, G/D BORDEAUX PARIS SAINT-GERMAIN **6**

OGC NICE **4**

LILLE LOSC **3**

SOCHAUX-M/B, FC SÈTE **2**

OLYMPIQUE LILLOIS, RCF PARIS, ROUBAIX-TOURCOING, STRASBOURG, AJ AUXERRE, RC LENS, MONTPELLIER **1**

1976 1977 1978 1979 1980 1981 1982 1983 1984 1985 1986 1987 1988 1989 1990 1991 1992 1993 1994 1995 1996 1997 1998 1999 2000 2001 2002 2003 2004 2005 2006 2007 2008 2009 2010 2011 2012 2013 2014 2015 2016 2017

AFC ASIAN CUP TROPHIES AND GOALS

The most recent AFC Asian Cup in 2015 crowned host nation Australia the Champions of Asia after defeating the Republic of Korea 2–1 after extra time. The next tournament in 2019, which is to be hosted by the United Arab Emirates, will see the possible number of national teams expand from 16 to 24. The Asian Cup is the world's second oldest continental football championship, after Copa América, and the cup's most consistent side to date is Japan, who have triumphantly held the trophy aloft in four out of seven tournaments since 1992.

IRAN

119
37
3

KOREA REPUBLIC

100
32
2

CHINA PR

86
21

JAPAN

80
24
4

SAUDI ARABIA
63
19
3

KUWAIT
47
15
1

IRAQ
38
13
1

UZBEKISTAN
35
11

AUSTRALIA
34
10
1

UNITED ARAB EMIRATES
33
12

QATAR
33
6

ISRAEL
28
9
1

BAHRAIN
26
4

SYRIA
17
7

THAILAND
15
1

DPR KOREA
14
3

JORDAN
13
4

INDONESIA
10
2

HONG KONG
9

INDIA
8
2

KHMER REPUBLIC
8
1

SOUTH VIETNAM
8

MALAYSIA
7
1

OMAN
6
2

MYANMAR
5
2

TURKMENISTAN
4

VIETNAM
4
1

LEBANON
3

SINGAPORE
3
1

BANGLADESH
2

PALESTINE
1

● **TOURNAMENTS WON**
● **MATCHES WON**
● **GOALS SCORED**

100 INTERNATIONAL CAPS

At Wembley Stadium, on 11 April 1959, England captain Billy Wright became the first footballer to make 100 appearances for his country, but since then this feat has been repeated by many players around the world. The modern game's proliferation of matches (major nations play more games a year than their pre-1990s counterparts) and multiple substitution rules give today's players a better chance of becoming Centurions and also accounts for the absence in the list of such greats as Pelé (92 appearances), Diego Maradona (91), Eusébio (64) and Johan Cruyff (48).

Player	Country	Caps
Ahmed Hassan	Egypt	184
Hossam Hassan	Egypt	178
Claudio Suárez	Mexico	177
Mohamed Al-Deayea	Saudi Arabia	172
Iván Hurtado	Ecuador	168
Gianluigi Buffon	Italy	168
Iker Casillas	Spain	167
Vitalijs Astafjevs	Latvia	165
Cobi Jones	United States	164
Mohammed Al-Khilaiwi	Saudi Arabia	163
Adnan Al-Talyani	United Arab Emirates	161
Bader Al-Mutawa	Kuwait	158
Landon Donovan	United States	157
Sami Al-Jaber	Saudi Arabia	156
Martin Reim	Estonia	156
Essam El-Hadary	Egypt	153
Yasuhito Endo	Japan	152
Lothar Matthäus	West Germany / Germany	150
Salman Isa	Bahrain	149
Ali Daei	Iran	149
Javad Nekounam	Iran	148
Younis Mahmoud	Iraq	148
Robbie Keane	Republic of Ireland	146
Mohammed Husain	Bahrain	145
Pável Pardo	Mexico	145
Paulo da Silva	Paraguay	144
Anatoliy Tymoshchuk	Ukraine	144
Javier Zanetti	Argentina	143
Gerado Torrado	Mexico	143
Fawzi Doorbeen	Oman	143
Thomas Ravelli	Sweden	143
Anders Svensson	Sweden	143
Cafu	Brazil	142
Marko Kristal	Estonia	142
Lilan Thuram	France	142
Sergio Ramos	Spain	142
Abdullah Zubromawi	Saudi Arabia	141
Ahmed Mubarek	Oman	140
Giorgos Karagounis	Greece	139
Cristiano Ronaldo	Portugal	138
Rigobert Song	Cameroon	137
Jari Litmanen	Finland	137
Miroslav Klose	Germany	137
Amado Guevara	Honduras	137
Hussein Saeed	Iraq	137
Rafael Márquez	Mexico	137
Javier Mascherano	Argentina	136
Maynor Figueroa	Honduras	136
Fabio Cannavaro	Italy	136
Hong Myung-Bo	South Korea	136
Walter Centeno	Costa Rica	135
Noel Valladares	Honduras	135
Amer Shafi	Jordan	135
Waleed Ali Jumah	Kuwait	135
Andrés Guardado	Mexico	135
Daniel Bennett	Singapore	135
Darijo Srna	Croatia	134
Shay Given	Republic of Ireland	134
Dorinel Munteanu	Romania	134
Hussein Sulaimani	Saudi Arabia	134
Shahril Bin Ishak	Singapore	134
Jeff Agoos	United States	134
Andres Oper	Estonia	133
Carlos Ruiz	Guatemala	133
Bashar Abdullah	Kuwait	133
Saud Kariri	Saudi Arabia	133
Xavi	Spain	133
Andreas Isaksson	Sweden	133
Clint Dempsey	United States	132
Gabriel Gómez	Panama	131
Kim Källström	Sweden	131
Lee Woon-Jae	South Korea	131
Piatisuk Senamuang	Thailand	131
Sargis Hovseyan	Armenia	130
Lukas Podolski	Germany	130
Edwin van der Sar	Netherlands	130
Baihakki Bin Khaizan	Singapore	130
Michael Bradley	United States	130
Jorge Campos	Mexico	130
Roberto Palacios	Peru	129
Juan Arango	Venezuela	128
Dennis Rommedahl	Denmark	127
Ali Karimi	Iran	127
Linval Dixon	Jamaica	127
Luís Figo	Portugal	127
Lee Young-Pyo	South Korea	127
Marcelo Balboa	United States	127
Luis Marin	Costa Rica	126
Paolo Maldini	Italy	126
Wesley Sneijder	Netherlands	126
Ali Al-Habsi	Oman	126
Andoni Zubizarreta	Spain	126
Roberto Carlos	Brazil	125
Ibrahim Hassan	Egypt	125
Peter Shilton	England	125
Musaed Neda	Kuwait	125
Mario Fick	Liechtenstein	125
Peter Jehle	Liechtenstein	125
Petr Cech	Czech Republic	124
Hany Ramzy	Egypt	124
Ian Goodison	Jamaica	124
Jaime Penedo	Panama	124
Gheorghe Hagi	Romania	124
DaMarcus Beasley	United States	124
Thierry Henry	France	123
Didier Zokora	Ivory Coast	123
Michael Mifsud	Malta	123
Server Djeparov	Uzbekistan	123
Masami Ihara	Japan	122
Carlos Salcido	Mexico	122
Amad Al-Hosni	Oman	122
Ismail Matar	United Arab Emirates	122
Peter Schmeichel	Denmark	121
Walter Ayoví	Ecuador	121
Enar Jääger	Estonia	121
Bastian Schweinsteiger	Germany	121
Mohamed Abd Al-Jawad	Saudi Arabia	121
Osama Al-Hawsawi	Saudi Arabia	121
Aide Iskandar	Singapore	121
Ahmed Fathi	Egypt	120
Mart Poom	Estonia	120
Sergei Ignashevich	Russia	120
Yoo Sang-Chul	South Korea	120
Rüstü Reçber	Turkey	120
Subait Khater Al-Junaibi	United Arab Emirates	120
Wayne Rooney	England	119
Theodoros Zagorakis	Greece	119
Boniek García	Honduras	119
David Carabott	Malta	119
Gilbert Agius	Malta	119
Ramón Ramirez	Mexico	119
Cuauhtémoc Blanco	Mexico	119
Pat Jennings	Northern Ireland	119
Justo Villar	Paraguay	119
Cha-Bum-Kun	South Korea	119
Timur Kapadze	Uzbekistan	119
Heinz Hermann	Switzerland	118
Geremi	Cameroon	118
Samuel Eto'o	Cameroon	118
Karel Poborský	Czech Republic	118
Kolo Touré	Ivory Coast	118
Maxi Pereira	Uruguay	118
Lionel Messi	Argentina	117
Amer Khalil	Jordan	117
Sebastián Soria	Qatar	117
Mohammed Al-Shalhoub	Saudi Arabia	117
Olof Mellberg	Sweden	117
Ragnar Klavan	Estonia	116
Marcel Desailly	France	116
Kostas Katsouranis	Greece	116
Andrea Pirlo	Italy	116
Theodore Whitmore	Jamaica	116
Yoshikatsu Kawaguchi	Japan	116
John O'Shea	Republic of Ireland	116
Majed Abdullah	Saudi Arabia	116
Ahmed Madani	Saudi Arabia	116
Taisir Al-Jassim	Saudi Arabia	116
Andrés Iniesta	Spain	116
Roland Nilsson	Sweden	116
Zlatan Ibrahimovic	Sweden	116
Roberto Ayala	Argentina	116
David Beckham	England	115
Noureddine Naybet		115
Gheorghe Popescu		115
Khairul Amri	Singapore	115
Shunmugham Subramani		115
Abdulraheem Jumaa		115
Stipe Pletikosa	Croatia	114
Steven Gerrard	England	114
Kristen Viikmäe	Estonia	114
Raio Piiroja	Estonia	114

Caps	Player	Country
114	Nawaf Al-Khaldi	Kuwait
113	Martin Stocklasa	Liechtenstein
112	Edison Méndez	Ecuador
112	Yasser Al-Qahtani	Saudi Arabia
111	Nashat Akram	Iraq
110	Mehdi Mahdavikia	Iran
109	Mark Schwarzer	Australia
108	Alvaro Saborio	Costa Rica
108	Stern John	Trinidad & Tobago
107	Jalal Hosseini	Iran
106	Hao Haidong	PR China
106	Eric Wynalda	United States
105	Sami Hyypiä	Finland
104	Per Mertesacker	Germany
103	Stéphane Chapuisat	Switzerland
103	Mohammed Al-Jahani	Saudi Arabia
102	Hani Al-Dhabit	Oman
102	Savo Milošević	Fr Yugoslavia/Serbia & Montenegro/Serbia
101	Ulises De La Cruz	Ecuador
101	Thorbjørn Svensson	Norway
100	Dani Alves	Brazil
100	Levan Kobiashvili	Georgia
100	Igors Stepanovs	Latvia
100	Nazri Bin Nasir	
114	Khaled Al-Muwallid	Saudi Arabia
113	Ahmad Al-Dossari	Saudi Arabia
112	Abdel-Zaher El-Saqua	Egypt
112	Hakan Sükür	Turkey
111	Jarah Al-Ataiqi	Kuwait
110	Yuli Nakazawa	Japan
109	Sayed Mohammed Jaffer	Bahrain
108	Thomas Helveg	Denmark
108	Diego Godin	Uruguay
107	Jamal Mubarak	Kuwait
106	Frank Lampard	England
106	Joseph Musonda	Zambia
105	Imants Bleidelis	Latvia
104	Gustavo Cabrera	Guatemala
103	Andreas Herzog	Austria
103	Hwang Sun-Hong	South Korea
102	Román Torres	Panama
102	Dejan Stankovic	Fr Yugoslavia/Serbia & Montenegro/Serbia
101	Ahmed Shobair	Egypt
101	Luis Tejada	Peru
100	Robinho	Brazil
100	Angelos Basinas	Greece
100	Goce Sedloski	Macedonia
100	Park Ji-Sung	
114	Indra Sahdan Daud	Singapore
113	Xabi Alonso	Spain
112	Daniele De Rossi	Italy
112	Zuhair Bakheet	United Arab Emirates
111	Blas Pérez	Panama
110	Carmel Busuttil	Malta
109	Mauricio Solís	Costa Rica
108	Álex Aguinaga	Ecuador
108	Carlos Bocanegra	United States
107	Miroslav Karhan	Slovakia
106	Dmitri Kruglov	Estonia
106	Ildefons Lima	Andorra
105	Franz Burgmeier	Liechtenstein
104	Didier Drogba	Ivory Coast
103	Faouzi Aaish	Bahrain
103	Lee Dong-Gook	South Korea
102	Michał Żewłakow	Poland
102	Christopher Katongo	Zambia
101	József Bozsik	Hungary
101	László Bölöni	Romania
100	Dario Šimic	Croatia
100	Carlos Pavón	Honduras
100	Henning Berg	Norway
100	Carles Puyol	
114	Björn Nordqvist	Sweden
113	Angus Eve	Trinidad & Tobago
112	Dino Zoff	Italy
112	Diego Forlán	Uruguay
111	Cesc Fàbregas	Spain
110	John Arne Riise	Norway
109	Hawar Mulla Mohammed	Iraq
108	Zinedine Zidane	France
108	Jürgen Klinsmann	West Germany/Germany
107	Aaron Mokoena	South Africa
106	Guillermo Ramírez	Guatemala
105	Óscar Sonejee	Andorra
105	Khamis Al-Dosari	Saudi Arabia
104	Makoto Hasebe	Japan
103	Ioannis Okkas	Cyprus
103	Franz Beckenbauer	West Germany
102	Steve Staunton	Republic of Ireland
102	Husain Ahmed	Bahrain
101	Andranik Teymourian	Iran
101	Vasiliy Berezutskiy	Russia
100	Hans-Jurgen Dörner	East Germany
100	Rúnar Kristinsson	Iceland
100	Román Torres	Panama
100	Piyapong Pue-on	
114	Abdulla Al-Mazooqi	Bahrain
113	Tim Howard	United States
112	Juris Laizans	Latvia
112	Carlos Valderrama	Colombia
111	David Silva	Spain
110	Carlos Gamarra	Paraguay
109	Rafael van der Vaart	Netherlands
108	Gábor Király	Hungary
107	Ahmed El-Kass	Egypt
107	Henrik Larsson	Sweden
106	Shinji Okazaki	Japan
105	Lúcio	Brazil
105	Radhi Jaïdi	Tunisia
104	Mihails Zeminskis	Latvia
103	Michael Laudrup	Denmark
103	Mario Yepes	Colombia
102	Kenny Dalglish	Scotland
101	Alyaksandr Kulchy	Belarus
101	Joe Brincat	Malta
101	Oleg Blokhin	Soviet Union
100	Ulf Kirsten	East Germany/Germany
100	Emad Mohammed	Iraq
100	Roberto Acuña	Paraguay
100	Joe-Max Moore	
113	Viktor Onopko	CIS/Russia
113	Alain Geiger	Switzerland
112	Frank de Boer	Netherlands
112	Hussain Ali Baba	Bahrain
111	Andriy Shevchenko	Ukraine
110	Fernando Couto	Portugal
109	Niclas Alexandersson	Sweden
108	Nohayr Al-Mutairi	Kuwait
107	Bobby Moore	England
107	Diego Simeone	Argentina
106	Francisco Javier Rodríguez	Mexico
105	Stiliyan Petrov	Bulgaria
105	Jürgen Kohler	West Germany / Germany
104	Dirk Kuyt	Netherlands
103	Indrek Zelinski	Estonia
102	Ivica Olic	Croatia
102	Raúl	Spain
101	Taffarel	Brazil
101	Phillip Cocu	Netherlands
101	Kasey Keller	United States
100	Luis Capurro	Ecuador
100	Siaka Tiéné	Ivory Coast
100	Denis Caniza	Paraguay
100	Earnie Stewart	
113	Philipp Lahm	Germany
112	Li Weifeng	PR China
112	Roque Santa Cruz	Paraguay
111	Rolando Fonseca	Costa Rica
111	Abdulsalam Jumaa	United Arab Emirates
110	Kevin Kilbane	Republic of Ireland
109	Totchtawan Sripan	Thailand
108	Alberto García Aspe	Mexico
107	Ashley Cole	England
106	Rashad Sadygov	Azerbaijan
106	Giovanni van Bronckhorst	Netherlands
105	Tomáš Rosický	Czech Republic
105	Josip Šimunic	Croatia
104	Aaron Hughes	Northern Ireland
103	Didier Deschamps	France
102	Martin Jørgensen	Denmark
102	Bülent Korkmaz	Turkey
101	Gonzalo Jara	Chile
101	Robin van Persie	Netherlands
101	Thomas Sørenson	Denmark
100	Mohamed Aboutrika	Egypt
100	Yaya Toure	Ivory Coast
100	Jorge Soto	Peru
100	Tony Meola	
113	Ali Hussein Rehema	Iraq
112	Yénier Márquez	Cuba
112	Claudio Bravo	Spain
111	Odelín Molina	Cuba
111	Claudio Reyna	United States
110	Fernando Torres	Spain
109	José Rey	Venezuala
108	Bilal Mohammed	Qatar
107	Joel Lindpere	Estonia
106	Ismail Abdul-Latif	Bahrain
106	Nani	Portugal
105	Bobby Charlton	England
104	Nader El-Sayed	Egypt
104	Héctor Chumpitaz	Peru
103	Mahdi Kareem	Iraq
102	Aleksandr Dmitrijev	Estonia
102	Mohamed Omar	United Arab Emirates
101	Leonel Álvarez	Colombia
101	Vincent Enyeama	Nigeria
101	Elijah Tana	Zambia
100	Ari Hjelm	Finland
100	Donovan Rcketts	Jamaica
100	Grzegorz Lato	Poland
113	Andrejs Rubi…	Latvia
112	Jon Dahl Tomasson	Denmark
112	Wesam Abdulmajid	Qatar
111	Wael Gomaa	Egypt
111	Kennedy Mw…	Zambia
110	Paul Caligiuri	United States
109	Alexis Sanch…	Chile
108	R.zvan Ra…	Romania
107	Patrick Vieira	France
106	Fan Zhiyi	PR China
106	Muhsin Mus…	United Arab Em…
105	Jonatan Johansson	Finland
104	Billy Wright	England
104	Kim Tae-You…	South Korea
103	Máris Verpakovski…	Latvia
102	Joseph Kam…	Malawi
102	Jozy Altidor…	USA
101	Thomas Hä…	West Germa… Germany
101	Joseph Yob…	Nigeria
101	Lakhdar Be…	Algeria
100	Didier Ovon…	Gabon
100	Fahad Awad…	Kuwait
100	Damien Du…	Republic of I…

LIGUE 1 GAME WINS

Ligue 1 began in 1932, switching to its current name in 2002. Although many view it as one of the weaker of the major European leagues, it is one of the most evenly contested. Until Monaco's 2017 triumph, PSG have recently held sway, but in modern times AS Saint-Etienne (League 1's most successful club), Olympique Lyon (winner of a record seven consecutive titles between 2002 and 2008) and Olympique de Marseille (most seasons and wins in top flight) have all dominated the league.

Club	Wins
SO MONTPELLIER	104
CO ROUBAIX	130
AJACCIO	131
GUINGAMP	133
TOULON	134
BREST	140
STADE FRANÇAIS	143
LORIENT	146
TROYES	151
LAVAL	157
RED STAR	168
FC NANCY	181
CAEN	183
SÈTE	198
ROUEN	233
CANNES	246
LE HAVRE	257
TOULOUSE FC	269
SEDAN	291
ANGERS	310
MONTPELLIER	315
TOULOUSE	345
NANCY	375
VALENCIENNES	375
RC PARIS	426
BASTIA	434
NIMES	482
AUXERRE	483
REIMS	523
STRASBOURG	690
METZ	709
RENNES	738

Source: Opta (May 2017)

Under 100 Wins

OLYMPIQUE LILLOIS **98**	ALÈS **42**	CA PARIS **13**	AVIGNON **7**
FIVES **77**	LIMOGES **37**	COLMAR **12**	BOULOGNE-SUR-MER **7**
EXCELSIOR **75**	PARIS FC **31**	LYON OU **11**	AIX **6**
ANTIBES **65**	ANGOULÊME **30**	NIORT **11**	ISTRES **6**
LE MANS **65**	GRENOBLE **30**	BÉZIERS **9**	CLUB FRANCAIS **5**
MULHOUSE **51**	MARTIGUES **27**	CHÂTEAUROUX **8**	HYÈRES **4**
ÉVIAN TG **45**	RC ROUBAIX **26**	GUEUGNON **8**	ARLES-AVIGNON **3**
TOURS **44**	DIJON **17**	GFC AJACCIO **8**	

PARIS SAINT-GERMAIN **747**

RC LENS **770**

NICE **780**

NANTES **788**

LILLE **794**

SOCHAUX **859**

OLYMPIQUE LYONNAIS **908**

MONACO **955**

SAINT-ÉTIENNE **1001**

BORDEAUX **1021**

MARSEILLE **1058**

2010 WORLD CUP GOALS

The 2010 World Cup in South Africa was the first to be hosted on African soil. To the background blast of thousands of vuvuzelas, it was Ghana and Uruguay who were the surprise packages – separated only by penalties in the quarter-final, after Luis Suárez's villainous last-minute handball save. Spain would triumph over Netherlands in the final of a tournament illuminated by goals such as the incredible effort from an impossible angle by Brazil's Maicon, a precision chip from Italy's Fabio Quagliarella and, most memorable of all, the powerful left-foot punt from South Africa's Siphiwe Tshabalala...

SIPHIWE TSHABALALA – South Africa vs Mexico

Siphiwe Tshabalala belts the ball hard from the 18-yard box to take South Africa into the lead against Mexico, 11 June 2010.

1. Flick-on **dos Santos**
2. Interception **Mokoena**
3. Ball recovery **Letsholonyane**
4. Pass **Letsholonyane**
5. Pass **Dikgacoi**
6. Pass **Mphela**
7. Through ball **Dikgacoi**
8. Goal **Tshabalala**

KEY

| Ball movement | ——— | Player with ball | ············ |
| Shot | ——⚽ | Player without ball | ··············· |

MAICON – Brazil vs DPR Korea

1. Throw in **Silva**
2. Pass (long ball, chipped) **Melo**
3. Pass **Elano**
4. Goal **Maicon**

MESUT ÖZIL – Germany vs Ghana

1. Pass **Lahm**
2. Pass **Müller**
3. Pass **Lahm**
4. Pass **Müller**
5. Goal **Özil**

FABIO QUAGLIARELLA – Italy vs Slovakia

1. Launch (long ball) **Škrtel**
2. Ball recovery **Chiellini**
3. Pass **Chiellini**
4. Pass **Marchetti**
5. Lay-off **Cannavaro**
6. Pass **Chiellini**
7. Pass **Pirlo**
8. Lay-off **Quagliarella**
9. Pass (chipped, long ball) **Pirlo**
10. Pass **Maggio**
11. Clearance **Zabavnik**
12. Pass **Pirlo**
13. Blocked **De Rossi**
14. Block **Kopúnek**
15. Pass **De Rossi**
16. Goal **Quagliarella**

GIOVANNI VAN BRONCKHORST – Netherlands vs Uruguay

1. Pass (long ball) **Kuyt**
2. Pass **de Zeeuw**
3. Pass **Sneijder**
4. Pass **de Zeeuw**
5. Goal **Van Bronckhorst**

Source: Opta (October 2015)

MOST SUCCESSFUL EUROPEAN MANAGERS SINCE 1960

1	**Bob Paisley**	
2	**Carlo Ancelotti**	
3	**Alex Ferguson**	
4	**Helenio Herrera**	
5	**José Mourinho**	
6	**Nereo Rocco**	
7	**José Villalonga**	
8	**Luis Carniglia**	
9	**Ottmar Hitzfeld**	
10	**Miguel Muñoz**	

Source: Google (June 2017)
Super cups and careers outside Europe not included

No matter how wealthy the club, it is a magnificent feat to guide a club to a league title. It is something else to take them to European success. Repeating the achievement takes a coach to legendary status. Separating the greatest from the great, however, is a tougher call. How do we rank Bob Paisley's European and League titles against Helenio Herrera's record? And, how much greater an achievement are the against-the-odds European triumphs of José Mourinho's Porto or Jock Stein's Celtic?

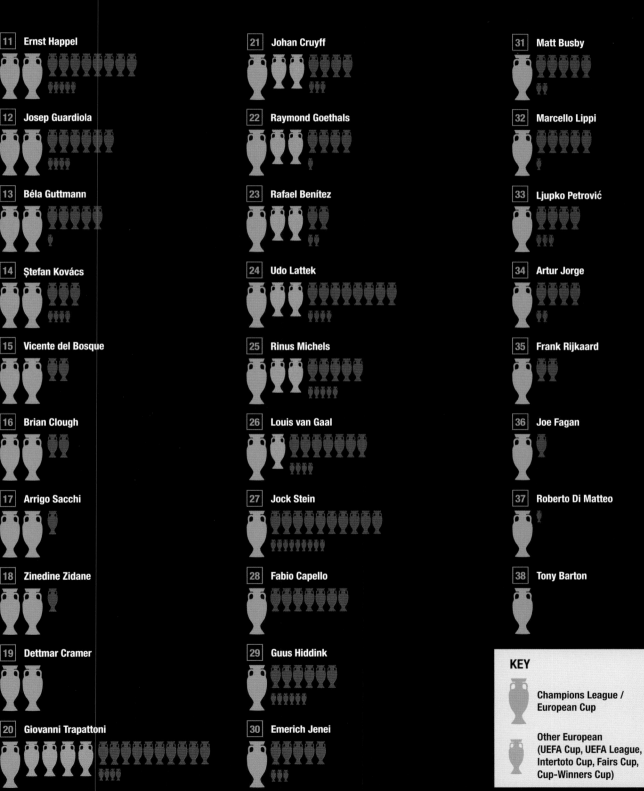

11 Ernst Happel

12 Josep Guardiola

13 Béla Guttmann

14 Ştefan Kovács

15 Vicente del Bosque

16 Brian Clough

17 Arrigo Sacchi

18 Zinedine Zidane

19 Dettmar Cramer

20 Giovanni Trapattoni

21 Johan Cruyff

22 Raymond Goethals

23 Rafael Benítez

24 Udo Lattek

25 Rinus Michels

26 Louis van Gaal

27 Jock Stein

28 Fabio Capello

29 Guus Hiddink

30 Emerich Jenei

31 Matt Busby

32 Marcello Lippi

33 Ljupko Petrović

34 Artur Jorge

35 Frank Rijkaard

36 Joe Fagan

37 Roberto Di Matteo

38 Tony Barton

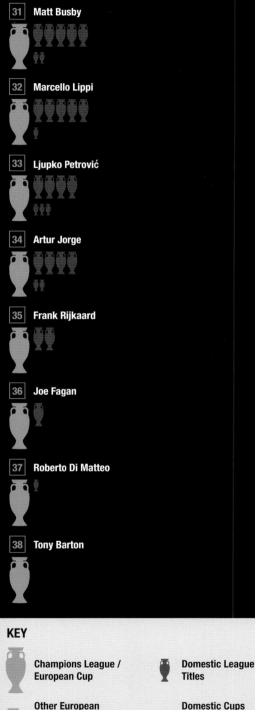

KEY

Champions League / European Cup

Other European (UEFA Cup, UEFA League, Intertoto Cup, Fairs Cup, Cup-Winners Cup)

Domestic League Titles

Domestic Cups (premier tournament in nation only e.g. FA Cup, Copa Del Rey, DFB Pokal)

LIGUE 1 GOALS PER CLUB

Seen by many of the world's richest clubs as a nursery for emerging young players, Ligue 1 has given renowned forwards such as Thierry Henry, Didier Drogba, Karim Benzema and Eden Hazard their first team breaks. Zlatan Ibrahimović, a rare star import to the league, hit 113 goals in just 122 Ligue 1 games, but left France long before catching record holder Delio Onnis (an Argentinian nicknamed "The Italian"!) who netted 299 goals in 449 appearances between 1972 and 1986.

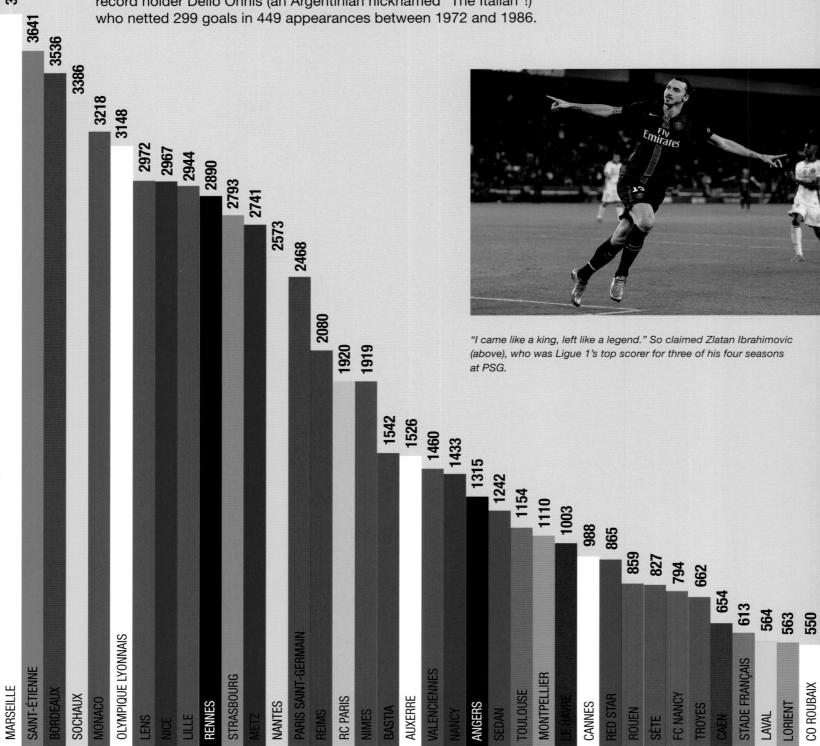

"I came like a king, left like a legend." So claimed Zlatan Ibrahimovic (above), who was Ligue 1's top scorer for three of his four seasons at PSG.

Club	Goals
MARSEILLE	3845
SAINT-ÉTIENNE	3641
BORDEAUX	3536
SOCHAUX	3386
MONACO	3218
OLYMPIQUE LYONNAIS	3148
LENS	2972
NICE	2967
LILLE	2944
RENNES	2890
STRASBOURG	2793
METZ	2741
NANTES	2573
PARIS SAINT-GERMAIN	2468
REIMS	2080
RC PARIS	1920
NIMES	1919
BASTIA	1542
AUXERRE	1526
VALENCIENNES	1460
NANCY	1433
ANGERS	1315
SEDAN	1242
TOULOUSE	1154
MONTPELLIER	1110
LE HAVRE	1003
CANNES	988
RED STAR	865
ROUEN	859
SÈTE	827
FC NANCY	794
TROYES	662
CAEN	654
STADE FRANÇAIS	613
LAVAL	564
LORIENT	563
CO ROUBAIX	550

DELIO ONNIS	299	BERNARD LACOMBE	255	HERVÉ REVELLI	216	ROGER COURTOIS	210
THADÉE CISOWSKI	206	ROGER PIANTONI	203	JOSEPH UJLAKI	190	FLEURY DI NALLO	187
CARLOS BIANCHI	179	GUNNAR ANDERSSON	179	HASSAN AKESBI	173	JEAN BARATTE	169
JUST FONTAINE	164	ALAIN GIRESSE	163	ANDRÉ GUY	159	DÉSIRÉ KORANYI	157
JEAN-PIERRE PAPIN	156	JACKY VERGNES	153	JOSIP SKOBLAR	151	LUCIEN COSSOU	149
DOMINIQUE ROCHETEAU	145	RACHID MEKHLOUFI	143	PAULETA	141	YVON DOUIS	140
MICHEL PLATINI	139	STÉPHANE BRUEY	139	SONNY ANDERSON	138	SALIF KEÏTA	135
HENRI HILTL	134	HÉCTOR DE BOURGOING	133	LILIAN LASLANDES	126	BAFÉTIMBI GOMIS	122
ZLATAN IBRAHIMOVIĆ	113	ALAIN CAVEGLIA	104	ANDRÉ-PIERRE GIGNAC	102	ALEXANDRE LACAZETTE	100
MAMADOU NIANG	100						

> **"I think that goalscoring is something that is born in a person – it's in the blood."**
>
> Jean-Pierre Papin

If ever there was a born goalscorer it was Papin. As Marseille's striker he was Ligue 1's top scorer in five consecutive seasons between 1988 and 1992. On returning to France from sojourns at Milan and Bayern, he carried on scoring at Bordeaux, taking his league tally to 156 goals in 270 appearances – the greatest goalscorer in modern French football.

Source: Opta (May 2017)
Seasons 1992–93 to 2016–17
Colour relates to the team for which the player scored the highest number of goals.

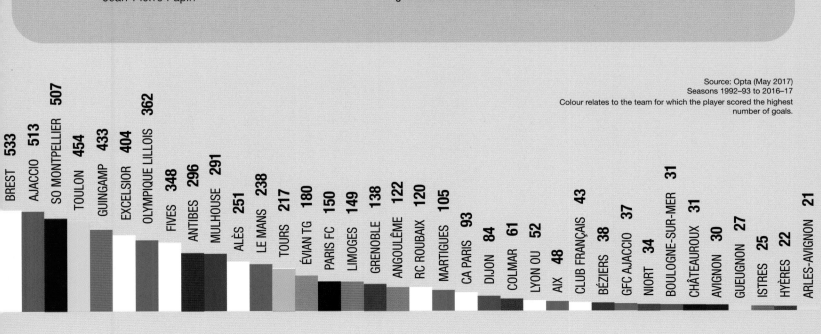

Team	Goals
BREST	533
AJACCIO	513
SO MONTPELLIER	507
TOULON	454
GUINGAMP	433
EXCELSIOR	404
OLYMPIQUE LILLOIS	362
FIVES	348
ANTIBES	296
MULHOUSE	291
ALÈS	251
LE MANS	238
TOURS	217
ÉVIAN TG	180
PARIS FC	150
LIMOGES	149
GRENOBLE	138
ANGOULÊME	122
RC ROUBAIX	120
MARTIGUES	105
CA PARIS	93
DIJON	84
COLMAR	61
LYON OU	52
AIX	48
CLUB FRANÇAIS	43
BÉZIERS	38
GFC AJACCIO	37
NIORT	34
BOULOGNE-SUR-MER	31
CHÂTEAUROUX	31
AVIGNON	30
GUEUGNON	27
ISTRES	25
HYÈRES	22
ARLES-AVIGNON	21

WORLD CUP FOULS AND CARDS

Behind these figures lie some of the most controversial and downright disgraceful moments in World Cup history. They include the South Africa vs Denmark tie in 1998, which resulted in seven yellow and three red cards, plus the three yellows in one match collected by Josip Šimunić for Croatia against Australia in 2006. If you thought that was bad, let's not forget the final itself, which saw two Argentinians sent off in 1990 and Zinedine Zidane seeing red after a confrontation with Marco Materazzi in 2006.

ARGENTINA 112	GERMANY 110	BRAZIL 95	ITALY 89	NETHERLANDS 89	MEXICO 67
SPAIN 65	URUGUAY 61	KOREA REPUBLIC 60	FRANCE 56	ENGLAND 50	USA 48
CAMEROON 45	CHILE 43	POLAND 40	PORTUGAL 40	PARAGUAY 39	SWEDEN 38
BELGIUM 37	GHANA 33	CROATIA 33	BULGARIA 33	ROMANIA 32	DENMARK 31
JAPAN 31	SWITZERLAND 31	COSTA RICA 30	TUNISIA 28	YUGOSLAVIA 27	NIGERIA 27
AUSTRIA 24	ECUADOR 23	AUSTRALIA 23	COLOMBIA 22	SAUDI ARABIA 22	USSR 21
SOUTH AFRICA 20	GREECE 19	SLOVENIA 19	MOROCCO 19	IVORY COAST 19	RUSSIA 19
IRAN 18	SERBIA 18	TURKEY 17	SCOTLAND 17	CZECHOSLOVAKIA 17	REPUBLIC OF IRELAND 16
ALGERIA 14	SENEGAL 14	HONDURAS 13	NORWAY 13	UKRAINE 12	SLOVAKIA 11
PERU 10	EAST GERMANY 10	ANGOLA 9	NORTHERN IRELAND 9	EL SALVADOR 9	TOGO 8
IRAQ 8	TRINIDAD AND TOBAGO 8	UNITED ARAB EMIRATES 6	BOLIVIA 6	NEW ZEALAND 6	CHINA PR 5
CZECH REPUBLIC 5	JAMAICA 4	EGYPT 4	HUNGARY 4	ISRAEL 4	HAITI 3
KUWAIT 3	BOSNIA AND HERZEGOVINA 3	DPR KOREA 2	ZAIRE 2	CANADA 1	

ARGENTINA 10 CAMEROON 8 URUGUAY 8 NETHERLANDS 7 ITALY 6 PORTUGAL 6

BRAZIL 6 MEXICO 6 FRANCE 6 GERMANY 5 CROATIA 4 USA 4

AUSTRALIA 4 ENGLAND 3 DENMARK 3 BELGIUM 3 BULGARIA 3 SWEDEN 3

SERBIA 3 ALGERIA 2 CHILE 2 TURKEY 2 KOREA REPUBLIC 2 BOLIVIA 2

PARAGUAY 2 HUNGARY 2 USSR 2 HONDURAS 2 CZECHOSLOVAKIA 2 SOUTH AFRICA 2

CZECH REPUBLIC 2 TUNISIA 1 CANADA 1 POLAND 1 JAMAICA 1 GREECE 1

SLOVENIA 1 TOGO 1 ANGOLA 1 UNITED ARAB EMIRATES 1 COSTA RICA 1 UKRAINE 1

IVORY COAST 1 SENEGAL 1 GHANA 1 IRAQ 1 YUGOSLAVIA 1 TRINIDAD AND TOBAGO 1

ZAIRE 1 SAUDI ARABIA 1 RUSSIA 1 ECUADOR 1 SCOTLAND 1 ROMANIA 1

SWITZERLAND 1 NORTHERN IRELAND 1 CHINA PR 1 AUSTRIA 1 NIGERIA 1 SPAIN 1

Total Fouls 1966–2014

GERMANY 1339	SWEDEN 467	SWITZERLAND 291	ALGERIA 205	TURKEY 117	TOGO 56
BRAZIL 1212	CAMEROON 438	COLOMBIA 284	MOROCCO 202	EL SALVADOR 109	EGYPT 52
ARGENTINA 1153	USSR 421	AUSTRIA 277	CZECHOSLOVAKIA 197	UKRAINE 108	CZECH REPUBLIC 52
ITALY 1147	PORTUGAL 399	ROMANIA 270	SAUDI ARABIA 184	SLOVENIA 103	ZAIRE 51
NETHERLANDS 996	USA 396	DENMARK 269	ECUADOR 184	SENEGAL 100	TRINIDAD AND TOBAGO 50
FRANCE 781	BULGARIA 383	COSTA RICA 252	SOUTH AFRICA 157	SERBIA 89	UNITED ARAB EMIRATES 48
ENGLAND 773	CHILE 357	AUSTRALIA 249	IVORY COAST 151	NEW ZEALAND 88	CANADA 45
SPAIN 735	PARAGUAY 348	IRAN 246	GREECE 150	DPR KOREA 86	BOSNIA AND HERZEGOVINA 41
MEXICO 683	YUGOSLAVIA 343	REPUBLIC OF IRELAND 238	NORTHERN IRELAND 150	ANGOLA 73	BOLIVIA 40
URUGUAY 652	JAPAN 319	TUNISIA 237	RUSSIA 141	SLOVAKIA 69	CHINA PR 40
BELGIUM 592	SCOTLAND 312	GHANA 233	HONDURAS 135	ISRAEL 68	HAITI 34
POLAND 574	NIGERIA 296	PERU 215	NORWAY 126	IRAQ 61	KUWAIT 32
KOREA REPUBLIC 516	CROATIA 291	HUNGARY 206	EAST GERMANY 119	JAMAICA 56	

Source: Opta (August 2015)

BUNDESLIGA GOALS PER CLUB

The German Bundesliga is the go-to league for goals with the highest goals per game ratio in Europe at 2.94 a game. As in all Bundesliga records, it's hard to ignore Bayern München. They are the only team to net 100 goals in a season (101 in 1971–72) and in Gerd Müller, seven-time leading goalscorer, they have arguably the game's greatest ever goal poacher. Among recent heroes stand Robert Lewandowski with his incredible five goals in nine minutes against VfL Wolfsburg in September 2015 and Borussia Dortmund's Pierre-Emerick Aubameyang whose 31 strikes in 2016–17 made him the first player to score over 30 goals in a season for 40 years.

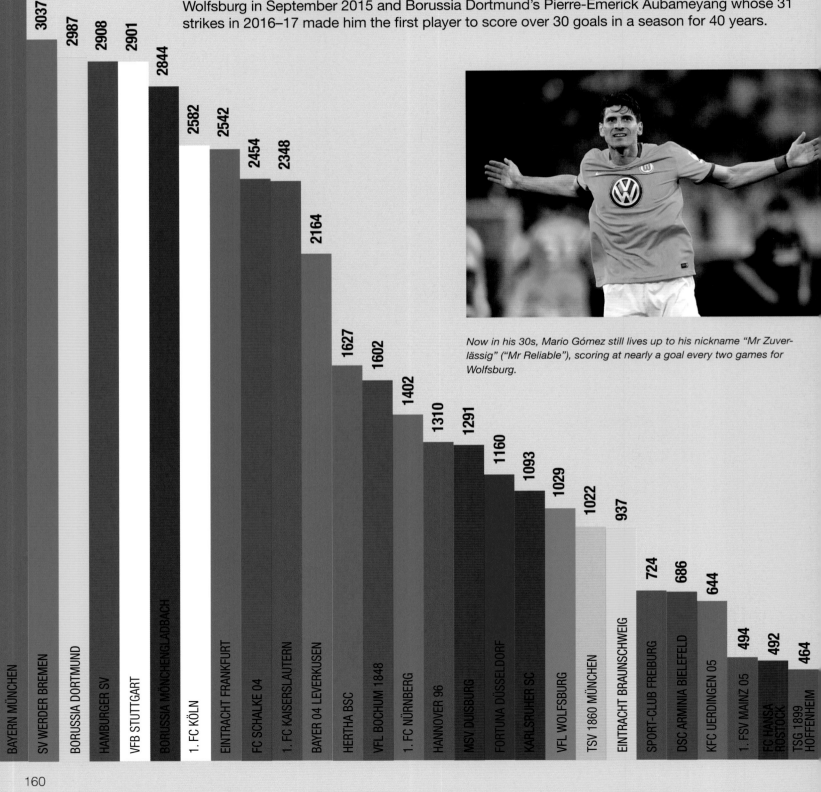

Now in his 30s, Mario Gómez still lives up to his nickname "Mr Zuver-lässig" ("Mr Reliable"), scoring at nearly a goal every two games for Wolfsburg.

Club	Goals
BAYERN MÜNCHEN	3853
SV WERDER BREMEN	3037
BORUSSIA DORTMUND	2987
HAMBURGER SV	2908
VFB STUTTGART	2901
BORUSSIA MÖNCHENGLADBACH	2844
1. FC KÖLN	2582
EINTRACHT FRANKFURT	2542
FC SCHALKE 04	2454
1. FC KAISERSLAUTERN	2348
BAYER 04 LEVERKUSEN	2164
HERTHA BSC	1627
VFL BOCHUM 1848	1602
1. FC NÜRNBERG	1402
HANNOVER 96	1310
MSV DUISBURG	1291
FORTUNA DÜSSELDORF	1160
KARLSRUHER SC	1093
VFL WOLFSBURG	1029
TSV 1860 MÜNCHEN	1022
EINTRACHT BRAUNSCHWEIG	937
SPORT-CLUB FREIBURG	724
DSC ARMINIA BIELEFELD	686
KFC UERDINGEN 05	644
1. FSV MAINZ 05	494
FC HANSA ROSTOCK	492
TSG 1899 HOFFENHEIM	464

GERD MÜLLER	365	KLAUS FISCHER	268	JUPP HEYNCKES	220	MANFRED BURGSMÜLLER	213
CLAUDIO PIZARRO	191	ULF KIRSTEN	182	STEFAN KUNTZ	179	KLAUS ALLOFS	177
DIETER MÜLLER	177	JOHANNES LÖHR	166	KARL-HEINZ RUMMENIGGE	162	BERND HÖLZENBEIN	160
FRITZ WALTER	157	MARIO GÓMEZ	154	ROBERT LEWANDOWSKI	151	THOMAS ALLOFS	148
BERND NICKEL	141	STEFAN KIESSLING	141	UWE SEELER	137	HORST HRUBESCH	136
GIOVANE ÉLBER	133	RUDI VÖLLER	132	MICHAEL ZORC	131	KARL ALLGÖWER	129
DIETER HOENESS	127	MARTIN MAX	126	GEORG VOLKERT	125	FRANK MILL	123
MIROSLAV KLOSE	121	HERBERT LAUMEN	121	LOTHAR MATTHÄUS	121	ROLAND WOHLFARTH	120
RONALD WORM	119	BERND RUPP	119	PIERRE LITTBARSKI	116	LOTHAR EMMERICH	115
REINER GEYE	113	KEVIN KURÁNYI	111	ANDREAS MÖLLER	110	JÜRGEN KLINSMANN	110
JÜRGEN GRABOWSKI	109	FREDI BOBIC	108	KLAUS TOPPMÖLLER	108	UWE RAHN	107
AÍLTON	106	STÉPHANE CHAPUISAT	106	CHRISTIAN SCHREIER	106	VEDAD IBIŠEVIĆ	104
BRUNO LABBADIA	103	MARCO BODE	101	THOMAS VON HEESEN	101		

Source: Opta (May 2017)

Colour relates to the team for which the player scored the highest number of goals.

Club	Goals
OFC KICKERS 1901	368
ROT-WEISS ESSEN	346
SV WALDHOF MANNHEIM	299
FC ST. PAULI	296
FC AUGSBURG	236
FC ENERGIE COTTBUS	211
1. FC SAARBRÜCKEN	202
ALEMANNIA AACHEN	186
SG WATTENSCHEID 09	186
ROT-WEISS OBERHAUSEN	182
SV DARMSTADT 98	152
WUPPERTALER SV	136
SG DYNAMO DRESDEN	132
BORUSSIA NEUNKIRCHEN	109
FC 08 HOMBURG	103
STUTTGARTER KICKERS	94
TENNIS BORUSSIA BERLIN	85
SPVGG UNTERHACHING	75
FC INGOLSTADT 04	69
RB LEIPZIG	66
FORTUNA KÖLN	46
BLAU-WEISS 90 BERLIN	36
SSV ULM 1846	36
SC PREUSSEN MÜNSTER	34
VFB LEIPZIG	32
SC PADERBORN 07	31
SPVGG GREUTHER FÜRTH	26
TASMANIA 1900 BERLIN	15

WOMEN'S WORLD CUP GOALSCORERS

Since Chinese defender Ma Li scored the first goal in Women's World Cup history, 770 goals have been scored in the finals. Among these are memorable strikes such as the stunning volley by Germany's Birgit Prinz in 2003 and Brazilian Marta's unstoppable flick and finish in 2007. The 2015 World Cup competition was graced by fabulous long-range shots from

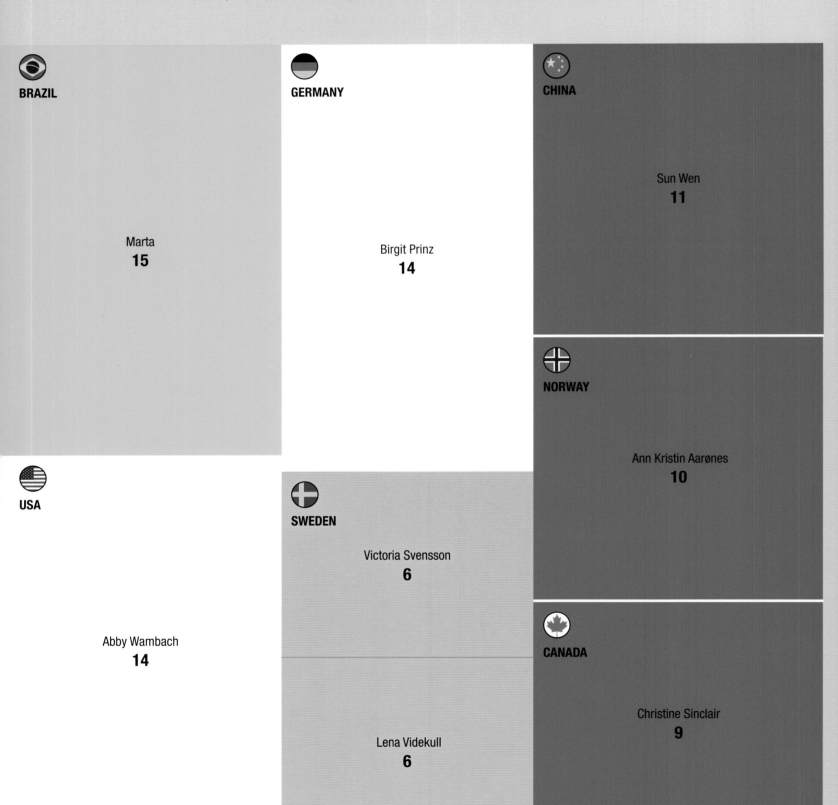

BRAZIL

Marta
15

USA

Abby Wambach
14

GERMANY

Birgit Prinz
14

SWEDEN

Victoria Svensson
6

Lena Videkull
6

CHINA

Sun Wen
11

NORWAY

Ann Kristin Aarønes
10

CANADA

Christine Sinclair
9

England's Lucy Bronze and France's Amandine Henry, but will surely be remembered most for the hat-trick by the USA's Carli Lloyd in the final, capped by a sensational right foot strike (and lob) from the halfway line. The goal was was awarded Goal of the Tournament.

Source: Opta (August 2015)

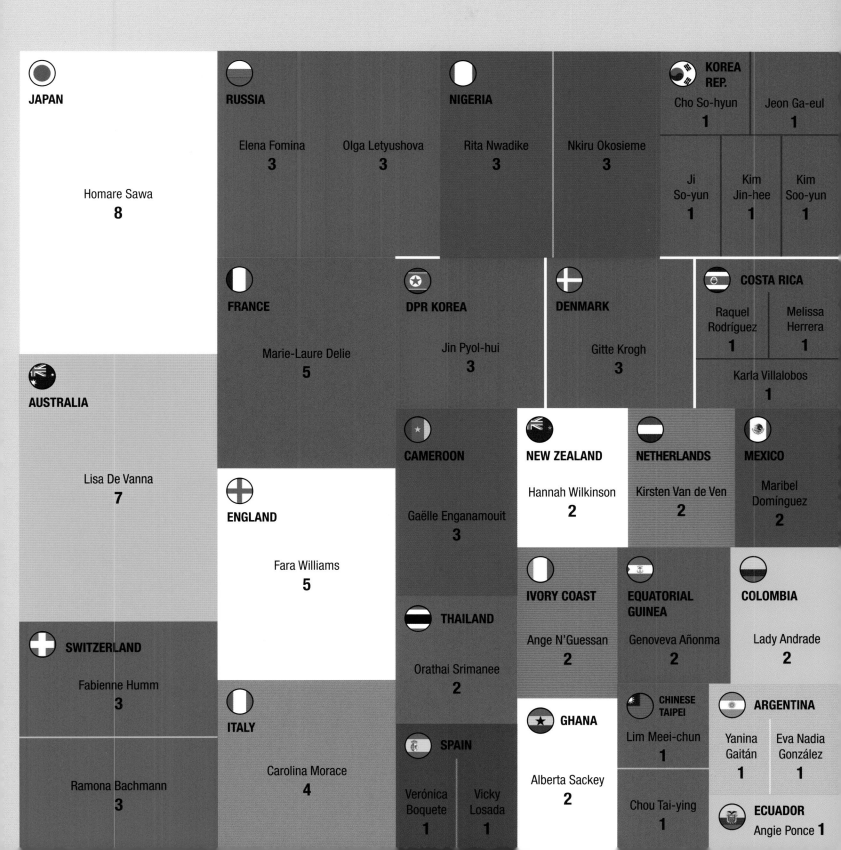

JAPAN

Homare Sawa
8

RUSSIA

Elena Fomina
3

Olga Letyushova
3

NIGERIA

Rita Nwadike
3

Nkiru Okosieme
3

KOREA REP.

Cho So-hyun
1

Jeon Ga-eul
1

Ji So-yun
1

Kim Jin-hee
1

Kim Soo-yun
1

FRANCE

Marie-Laure Delie
5

DPR KOREA

Jin Pyol-hui
3

DENMARK

Gitte Krogh
3

COSTA RICA

Raquel Rodríguez
1

Melissa Herrera
1

Karla Villalobos
1

AUSTRALIA

Lisa De Vanna
7

ENGLAND

Fara Williams
5

CAMEROON

Gaëlle Enganamouit
3

THAILAND

Orathai Srimanee
2

NEW ZEALAND

Hannah Wilkinson
2

NETHERLANDS

Kirsten Van de Ven
2

MEXICO

Maribel Domínguez
2

IVORY COAST

Ange N'Guessan
2

EQUATORIAL GUINEA

Genoveva Añonma
2

COLOMBIA

Lady Andrade
2

SWITZERLAND

Fabienne Humm
3

Ramona Bachmann
3

ITALY

Carolina Morace
4

SPAIN

Verónica Boquete
1

Vicky Losada
1

GHANA

Alberta Sackey
2

CHINESE TAIPEI

Lim Meei-chun
1

Chou Tai-ying
1

ARGENTINA

Yanina Gaitán
1

Eva Nadia González
1

ECUADOR

Angie Ponce **1**

MLS GAME WINS PER CLUB

The forerunner to the MLS was the ill-fated North American Soccer League (NASL), a division that relied too heavily on imported celebrity players such as Pelé and Franz Beckenbauer to have home success. The MLS too once enlisted the assistance of foreign stars to boost its appeal, including David Beckham, Cuauhtémoc Blanco, Andrea Pirlo and David Villa, but in recent years it has established itself as a sustainable league attracting an average of 18,600 fans a game, global TV interest and is dedicated to nurturing home-grown talent. Today, the MLS is the world's fastest-growing sport.

Source: Opta (October 2016)

Club	Wins
ORLANDO CITY SC	21
NEW YORK CITY FC	25
MIAMI FUSION	49
MONTREAL IMPACT	64
VANCOUVER WHITECAPS	68
PHILADELPHIA UNION	72
TAMPA BAY MUTINY	75
PORTLAND TIMBERS	77
CHIVAS USA	93
SPORTING KANSAS CITY	94
TORONTO FC	95
SAN JOSE EARTHQUAKES	98
SAN JOSE	122
SEATTLE SOUNDERS FC	134
HOUSTON DYNAMO	142
REAL SALT LAKE	150
KANSAS CITY WIZARDS	175
COLORADO RAPIDS	248

...ost recent major league in world football, the MLS is still
...ng. This table needs to be read in relation to the number of
...the team has been playing in the MLS. Although some clubs have
...their name, no teams have been relegated from the league.

...e original ten teams comprise: Colorado Rapids, Columbus
...C. United, Dallas Burn (later FC Dallas) , Kansas City Wizards, LA
...ew England Revolution, NY/NJ Metro Stars (later New York Red
...an Jose Clash (later Earthquakes) and Tampa Bay Mutiny.
...icago Fire, Miami Fusion

2005: Real Salt Lake, Chivas USA
2006: Houston Dynamo
2007: Toronto FC
2009: Seattle Sounders
2010: Philadelphia Union
2011: Portland Timbers, Vancouver Whitecaps
2012: Montreal Impact
2015: New York City FC, Orlando City
2017: Minnesota United, Atlanta United

CHICAGO FIRE **251**

NEW YORK RED BULLS **268**

COLUMBUS CREW SC **273**

FC DALLAS **275**

D.C. UNITED **279**

LA GALAXY **330**

AFRICA CUP OF NATIONS RECORDS BY NATION

The biennial African Cup of Nations tournament, contested by the nations of the Confederation of African Football, has been played since 1957. Just Egypt, Sudan and Ethiopia played the first two tournaments before it was enlarged to include four (1962), six (1963), eight (1968), 12 (1992) and then 16 teams (1996). Because of its apartheid policy South Africa was excluded from the competition until 1996. The tournament moved to odd-numbered years from 2013 to avoid conflict with the World Cup; this meant there were tournaments in consecutive years.

Senegal

Guinea-Bissau

Guinea

Sierra Leone

Liberia

Cape Verde

Cameroon celebrate winning the 2017 Africa Cup of Nations after the Indomitable Lions came from behind to beat Egypt 2–1 in Libreville, Gabon to seal a fifth tournament victory.

Qualified

0		12
1		13
2		14
3		15
4		16
5		17
6		18
7		19
8		20
9		21
10		22
11		23

Winner

Host

2014 WORLD CUP GOALS

There were too many unforgettable stories in Brazil's 2014 World Cup: reigning champions Spain crashing out in the group stage; the attacking zest displayed by Mexico, Costa Rica, USA and Colombia; Brazil's semi-final capitulation; and the superb football played by worthy winners Germany. Miroslav Klose was crowned the competition's top scorer, Colombia's James Rodríguez scored from a top-class chest, swivel and volley smash, Robin van Persie perfected a diving header and Mario Götze hit a volley worthy of winning a World Cup final.

ROBIN VAN PERSIE – Netherlands vs Spain

The Netherlands' Robin van Persie scores with his head to equalize in the match against Spain, 13 June 2014.

1. Throw in **Martins Indi**
2. Pass **De Jong**
3. Through ball (chipped, long ball) **Blind**
4. Goal (head) **Van Persie**

KEY

Ball movement ———	Player with ball ··············
Shot ———⚽	Player without ball ··············

MARIO GÖTZE – **Germany** vs Argentina

1. Free kick taken **Lahm**
2. Pass **Schweinsteiger**
3. Pass **Boateng**
4. Pass **Hummels**
5. Pass **Kroos**
6. Pass **Schürrle**
7. Pass **Kroos**
8. Pass (cross, chipped) **Schürrle**
9. Goal **Götze**

LIONEL MESSI – **Argentina** vs Bosnia

1. Free kick taken **Fernández**
2. Pass **Mascherano**
3. Pass **Di María**
4. Pass **Mascherano**
5. Pass **Gago**
6. Lay-off **Higuaín**
7. Pass **Messi**
8. Lay-off **Higuaín**
9. Take on **Messi**
10. Challenge **Bičakčić**
11. Goal **Messi**

JAMES RODRÍGUEZ – **Colombia** vs Uruguay

1. Pass **Armero**
2. Launch (long ball) **Ospina**
3. Head pass **González**
4. Pass (chipped, long ball) **Armero**
5. Head pass **Godín**
6. Pass (chipped) **Gutiérrez**
7. Pass **Aguilar**
8. Pass **Gutiérrez**
9. Pass **Cuadrado**
10. Pass **Zúñiga**
11. Pass **Gutiérrez**
12. Pass **Martínez**
13. Pass (cross, chipped) **Armero**
14. Head pass **Cuadrado**
15. Goal **Rodríguez**

DAVID VILLA – **Spain** vs Australia

1. Throw In (long ball) **McGowan**
2. Interception **Alonso**
3. Ball recovery **Iniesta**
4. Pass **Iniesta**
5. Pass **Torres**
6. Pass **Alonso**
7. Pass (long ball) **Cazorla**
8. Pass **Juanfran**
9. Pass **Iniesta**
10. Pass **Koke**
11. Pass **Alonso**
12. Pass **Cazorla**
13. Pass **Villa**
14. Pass (chipped, long ball) **Cazorla**
15. Pass **Juanfran**
16. Pass **Iniesta**
17. Pass **Juanfran**
18. Goal **Villa**

Source: Opta (October 2015)

UEFA EURO 2016 GOALS

Despite a record 108 goals being scored in the 2016 European Championship, the matches were not a feast of goals. With a ratio of just 2.12 a game, Euro 2016 was the lowest-scoring European Championship for 20 years. However, there certainly was drama: 18 goals (seven winners and three equalizers) were scored in the last five minutes or later, including Dimitri Payet's majestic 89th-minute winner against Romania in the opening game and Northern Ireland's Niall McGinn setting the record for latest goal ever in a European Championship at 96 minutes.

XHERDAN SHAQIRI – Switzerland vs Poland

Many believed Xherdan Shaqiri's acrobatic strike for Switzerland in their last-16 match against Poland to be the Goal of the Tournament.

1. Corner kick **Shaqiri**
2. Punch **Fabianski**
3. Blocked shot **Rodriguez**
4. Defensive block **Glik**
5. Pass **Fernandes**
6. Pass **Lichtsteiner**
7. Pass **Sommer**
8. Pass **Xhaka**
9. Pass **Shaqiri**
10. Unsuccessful pass **Rodriguez**
11. Blocked pass **Blaszczykowski**
12. Pass **Rodriguez**
13. Unsuccessful pass **Lichtsteiner**
14. Clearance **Pazdan**
15. Goal **Shaqiri**

KEY

Ball movement ——————   Player with ball ··············

Shot ————⚽   Player without ball ················

HAL ROBSON-KANU – Wales vs Belgium

1. Pass **Chester**
2. Pass **Gunter**
3. Pass **Bale**
4. Pass **Ramsey**
5. Take on **Robson-Kanu**
6. Unsuccessful challenge **Meunier**
7. Goal **Robson-Kanu**

ANTOINE GRIEZMANN – France vs Iceland

CRISTIANO RONALDO – Portugal vs Hungary

1. Pass **Patricio**
2. Pass **Carvalho**
3. Pass **Ronaldo**
4. Pass **Eliseu**
5. Pass **Carvalho**
6. Pass **Pepe**
7. Pass **Carvalho**
8. Pass **Patricio**
9. Pass **Pepe**
10. Pass **Vierinha**
11. Pass **Mario**
12. Pass **Nani**
13. Pass **Mario**
14. Goal **Ronaldo**

ROMELU LUKAKU – Belgium vs Republic of Ireland

FOOTBALL NATIONS

rations represent different regions of the world: UEFA (Europe), CAF
AF (North and Central America), CONMEBOL (South America), OFC
South Pacific island nations) and AFC (Asia). FIFA was founded on 21
by delegates from Belgium, Denmark, France, the Netherlands, Spain,
zerland. It now has more member countries than the United Nations – 208
he British nations, acting in unison, had a chequered relationship with the
early years, joining on 1906 but leaving on two occasions before re-joining
46.

SOCIATIONS:
UNDED

- UEFA
- OFC
- AFC
- CONMEBOL
- CONCACAF
- CAF

1921	Republic of Ireland
1922	Afghanistan
1922	Lithuania
1922	Peru
1923	Bulgaria
1923	Turkey
1924	China PR
1924	Colombia
1924	Cuba
1924	Grenada
1924	Uganda
1925	Bolivia
1925	Ecuador
1926	Greece
1926	Venezuela
1927	Mexico
1928	Antigua and Barbuda
1928	Bermuda
1928	Israel
1928	New Caledonia
1929	Zambia
1930	Albania
1930	Indonesia
1930	Tanzania
1931	Montenegro
1931	Nicaragua
1931	San Marino
1932	Aruba
1932	Lesotho
1932	St. Kitts and Nevis
1933	Cambodia
1933	Korea Republic
1933	Lebanon
1933	Malaysia
1934	Cyprus
1934	Liechtenstein
1934	Vanuatu
1935	El Salvador
1935	Honduras
1936	Chinese Tapei
1936	Liberia
1936	Sudan
1936	Syria
1936	Tajikistan
1937	India
1937	Panama
1938	Fiji
1938	Slovakia
1939	Macau
1939	Sri Lanka
1940	Puerto Rico
1943	Ethiopia
1945	Korea DPR
1945	Nigeria
1946	Kosovo

1946	Uzbekistan
1947	Iceland
1947	Myanmar
1948	Burundi
1948	FYR Macedonia
1948	Iraq
1948	Pakistan
1949	Jordan
1951	Laos
1951	Nepal
1951	Somalia
1952	Gambia
1952	Kuwait
1952	Mauritius
1953	Dominican Republic
1955	Morocco
1956	Saudi Arabia
1957	Bahrain
1957	Equatorial Guinea
1957	Ghana
1957	Tunisia
1959	Brunei Darussalam
1959	Cameroon
1959	Mongolia
1960	Burkino Faso
1960	Côte D'ivoire
1960	Guinea
1960	Kenya
1960	Mali
1960	Qatar
1960	Senegal
1960	Sierra Leone
1960	Togo
1961	Australia
1961	Central African Republic
1961	Madagascar
1961	Mauritania
1961	Niger
1962	DR Congo
1962	Algeria
1962	Benin
1962	Chad
1962	Gabon
1962	Libya
1962	Palestine
1962	Papua New Guinea
1962	Vietnam
1962	Yemen
1965	Tonga
1965	Zimbabwe
1966	Cayman Islands
1966	Malawi

1967	Bahamas
1968	Samoa
1968	Swaziland
1970	Botswana
1970	Dominica
1971	Cook Islands
1971	United Arab Emirates
1972	Bangladesh
1972	Rwanda
1974	British Virgin Islands
1974	Guinea-Bissau
1975	Guam
1975	São Tomé e Príncipe
1976	Mozambique
1978	Oman
1978	Solomon Islands
1979	Angola
1979	Comoros
1979	Djibouti
1979	Faroe Islands
1979	Seychelles
1979	St. Lucia
1979	St. Vincent and the Grenadines
1980	Belize
1982	Cape Verde Islands
1982	Maldives
1983	Bhutan
1984	American Samoa
1989	Belarus
1989	Tahiti
1990	Anguilla
1990	Georgia
1990	Moldova
1990	Namibia
1991	South Africa
1991	Ukraine
1992	Armenia
1992	Azerbaijan
1992	Bosnia and Herzegovina
1992	Kyrgystan
1992	Turkmenistan
1992	US Virgin Islands
1994	Andorra
1994	Montserrat
1996	Eritrea
1996	Turks and Caicos Islands
2002	Timor-Leste
2011	South Sudan

NATIONAL ASSOCIATIONS:
YEAR AFFILIATED WITH FIFA

1904
- Denmark
- Netherlands
- Belgium
- Switzerland
- Germany
- Sweden
- Spain
- France

- England
- Italy
- Austria

- Czech Republic
- Hungary

- Norway
- Finland

1910
- Scotland
- Wales
- Luxembourg

- Northern Ireland

- Argentina
- Russia

- Chile
- Canada

- USA

1920

- Japan

1934
- Haiti

- Curaçao
- Albania

- China PR

1930
- Phillipines

- Suriname
- Cuba
- Mexico
- Israel

- Costa Rica
- Greece

- Bolivia
- Ecuador

- Paraguay
- Thailand

- Peru
- Bulgaria

- Uruguay
- Brazil
- Egypt
- Portugal
- Poland
- Serbia

- Romania
- Estonia
- Latvia
- Republic of Ireland
- Lithuania
- Turkey

- Colombia
- Lebanon

- Syria

- El Salvador
- Panama

1938

1940

1950
- Nicaragua
- Iraq

- Venezuela
- Ethiopia
- Indonesia
- Sri Lanka
- Singapore
- Laos

- Jamaica
- Bermuda
- Somalia
- Cameroon
- Guinea

- Guatemala
- Honduras

- Iceland

- Cyprus
- Sudan
- New Zealand
- Korea Republic
- Afghanistan

- Iran
- India
- Myanmar
- Pakistan

- Australia

1962

1960

1954

- Hong Kong
- Cambodia
- Malaysia
- Chinese Tapei

1966
- Gabon
- Papua New Guinea

- Bahrain
- Barbados
- Bahamas
- Gambia
- Malawi

- Zimbabwe

- Fiji
- Kuwait
- Vietnam
- Trinidad and Tobago
- Congo DR
- Zambia
- Tanzania

- Lesotho
- Liberia
- Mauritius
- Burkino Faso
- Côte D'ivoire

- Mali
- Senegal
- Togo
- Central African Republic
- Madagascar

- Niger
- 84 Congo
- Algeria
- Benin
- Chad
- Libya

- Malta
- Puerto Rico
- Uganda
- Nigeria

- Morocco
- Tunisia
- Kenya
- Sierra Leone

1958
- Korea DPR
- Ghana
- Dominican Republic

- Jordan
- Saudi Arabia

- Guyana
- Mauritania

1970

- Equatorial Guinea
- Guinea-Bissau
- São Tomé e Principe
- Seychelles
- Cape Verde Islands
- Samoa
- Maldives
- Belize

1974
- United Arab Emirates

- Antigua and Barbuda
- Burundi
- Nepal
- Brunei Darussalam
- Qatar

- Liechtenstein
- Bangladesh

- Macau
- Swaziland
- Botswana
- Rwanda
- Grenada

1978
- St. Lucia
- St. Vincent and the Grenadines

1980
- Yemen
- Oman
- Angola
- Mozambique

1982

1986

- Vanuatu
- Solomon Islands
- Aruba
- San Marino
- Faroe Islands

- New Caledonia

2002

2000

- Bhutan

1998
- American Samoa
- Eritrea
- US Virgin Islands
- Turks and Caicos Islands
- Mongolia
- Palestine

- British Virgin Islands
- Montserrat
- Anguilla
- Guam
- Bosnia and Herzegovina
- Andorra

- Dominica
- Tonga
- Cook Islands
- Djibouti
- Turkmenistan
- Tajikistan
- Uzbekistan

1994

- Kyrgystan
- Slovakia
- FYR Macedonia
- Moldova
- Azerbaijan
- Kazakhstan

- St. Kitts and Nevis
- Cayman Islands
- Namibia
- South Africa
- Croatia

- Slovenia
- Belarus
- Georgia
- Ukraine
- Armenia

1990
- Tahiti

2006

- Comoros
- Timor-Leste

- Montenegro

2010

- South Sudan

2014

- Gibraltar
- Kosovo

Source: Opta (June 2017)

THE FOREIGN LEGION

The quest to build the best team in Europe now involves searching the globe for the best players. While cultural links still explain many of the sources – England picking the best Welsh, Scottish and Irish players, Germany looking to Switzerland and Austria, with Italy and Spain seeking out South American talent – all major clubs are now prepared to look further afield. Brazil is the leading provider of expatriates to Europe, with French players being most in demand across their own continent.

Source: Opta (August 2016–May 2017)

KEY:
- UEFA
- OFC
- AFC
- CONMEBOL
- CONCACAF
- CAF

Total number of players

Average number of appearances

ENGLISH PREMIER LEAGUE
177 ENGLISH PLAYERS

18.8 AVERAGE APPEARANCES IN SEASON • **3333** TOTAL APPEARANCES

347 FOREIGN PLAYERS
232   53   44   8   5   5

SPAIN	FRANCE	BELGIUM	NETHERLANDS
36	30	21	20
22.4	18.0	26.3	20.0
807	540	553	399

FRENCH LIGUE 1
303 FRENCH PLAYERS

18.7 AVERAGE APPEARANCES IN SEASON • **5652** TOTAL APPEARANCES

256 FOREIGN PLAYERS
126   79   42   6   3

GERMAN BUNDESLIGA
216 GERMAN PLAYERS

17.3 AVERAGE APPEARANCES IN SEASON • **3730** TOTAL APPEARANCES

253 FOREIGN PLAYERS
182   30   21   13   10   1

SWITZERLAND	AUSTRIA	BRAZIL	SPAIN
23	18	16	14
16.8	23.0	17.2	17.6
387	414	275	246

ITALIAN SERIE A
240 ITALIAN PLAYERS

17.9 AVERAGE APPEARANCES IN SEASON • **4301** TOTAL APPEARANCES

320 FOREIGN PLAYERS
175   99   38   4   3   1

BRAZIL
37
16.0
593

SPANISH LA LIGA
301 SPANISH PLAYERS

19.6 AVERAGE APPEARANCES IN SEASON • **5904** TOTAL APPEARANCES

240 FOREIGN PLAYERS
106   93   27   10   3   1

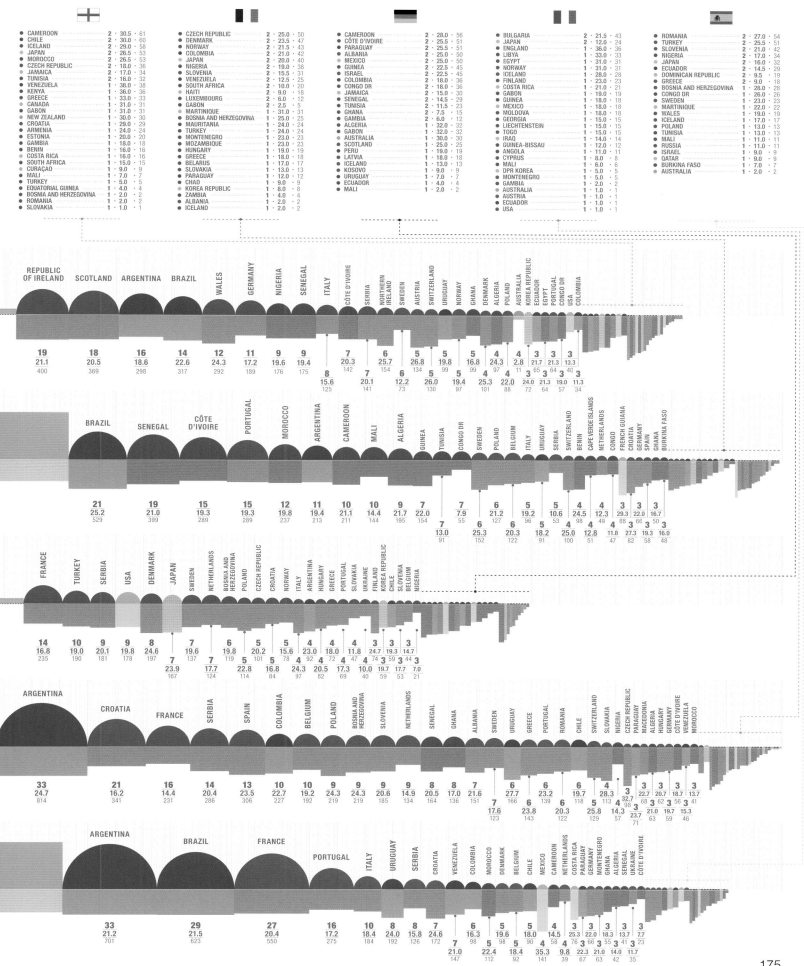

CAMEROON · 2 · 30.5 · 61
CHILE · 2 · 30.0 · 60
ICELAND · 2 · 29.0 · 58
JAPAN · 2 · 26.5 · 53
MOROCCO · 2 · 26.5 · 53
CZECH REPUBLIC · 2 · 18.0 · 36
JAMAICA · 2 · 17.0 · 34
TUNISIA · 2 · 16.0 · 32
VENEZUELA · 1 · 38.0 · 38
KENYA · 1 · 36.0 · 36
GREECE · 1 · 33.0 · 33
CANADA · 1 · 31.0 · 31
GABON · 1 · 31.0 · 31
NEW ZEALAND · 1 · 30.0 · 30
CROATIA · 1 · 29.0 · 29
ARMENIA · 1 · 24.0 · 24
ESTONIA · 1 · 20.0 · 20
GAMBIA · 1 · 18.0 · 18
BENIN · 1 · 16.0 · 16
COSTA RICA · 1 · 16.0 · 16
SOUTH AFRICA · 1 · 15.0 · 15
CURAÇAO · 1 · 9.0 · 9
MALI · 1 · 7.0 · 7
TURKEY · 1 · 5.0 · 5
EQUATORIAL GUINEA · 1 · 4.0 · 4
BOSNIA AND HERZEGOVINA · 1 · 2.0 · 2
ROMANIA · 1 · 2.0 · 2
SLOVAKIA · 1 · 1.0 · 1

CZECH REPUBLIC · 2 · 25.0 · 50
DENMARK · 2 · 23.5 · 47
NORWAY · 2 · 21.5 · 43
COLOMBIA · 2 · 21.0 · 42
JAPAN · 2 · 20.0 · 40
NIGERIA · 2 · 19.0 · 38
SLOVENIA · 2 · 15.5 · 31
VENEZUELA · 2 · 12.5 · 25
SOUTH AFRICA · 2 · 10.0 · 20
HAITI · 2 · 9.0 · 18
LUXEMBOURG · 2 · 6.0 · 12
GABON · 2 · 2.5 · 5
MARTINIQUE · 1 · 31.0 · 31
BOSNIA AND HERZEGOVINA · 1 · 25.0 · 25
MAURITANIA · 1 · 24.0 · 24
TURKEY · 1 · 24.0 · 24
MONTENEGRO · 1 · 23.0 · 23
MOZAMBIQUE · 1 · 23.0 · 23
HUNGARY · 1 · 19.0 · 19
GREECE · 1 · 18.0 · 18
BELARUS · 1 · 17.0 · 17
SLOVAKIA · 1 · 13.0 · 13
PARAGUAY · 1 · 12.0 · 12
CHAD · 1 · 9.0 · 9
KOREA REPUBLIC · 1 · 8.0 · 8
ZAMBIA · 1 · 4.0 · 4
ALBANIA · 1 · 2.0 · 2
ICELAND · 1 · 2.0 · 2

CAMEROON · 2 · 28.0 · 56
CÔTE D'IVOIRE · 2 · 25.5 · 51
PARAGUAY · 2 · 25.5 · 51
ALBANIA · 2 · 25.0 · 50
MEXICO · 2 · 25.0 · 50
GUINEA · 2 · 22.5 · 45
ISRAEL · 2 · 22.5 · 45
COLOMBIA · 2 · 18.0 · 36
CONGO DR · 2 · 18.0 · 36
JAMAICA · 2 · 15.0 · 30
SENEGAL · 2 · 14.5 · 29
TUNISIA · 2 · 11.5 · 23
GHANA · 2 · 7.5 · 15
GAMBIA · 2 · 6.0 · 12
ALGERIA · 1 · 32.0 · 32
GABON · 1 · 32.0 · 32
AUSTRALIA · 1 · 30.0 · 30
SCOTLAND · 1 · 25.0 · 25
PERU · 1 · 19.0 · 19
LATVIA · 1 · 18.0 · 18
ICELAND · 1 · 13.0 · 13
KOSOVO · 1 · 9.0 · 9
URUGUAY · 1 · 7.0 · 7
ECUADOR · 1 · 4.0 · 4
MALI · 1 · 2.0 · 2

BULGARIA · 2 · 21.5 · 43
JAPAN · 2 · 12.0 · 24
ENGLAND · 1 · 36.0 · 36
LIBYA · 1 · 33.0 · 33
EGYPT · 1 · 31.0 · 31
NORWAY · 1 · 31.0 · 31
ICELAND · 1 · 28.0 · 28
FINLAND · 1 · 23.0 · 23
COSTA RICA · 1 · 21.0 · 21
GABON · 1 · 19.0 · 19
GUINEA · 1 · 18.0 · 18
MEXICO · 1 · 18.0 · 18
MOLDOVA · 1 · 18.0 · 18
GEORGIA · 1 · 15.0 · 15
LIECHTENSTEIN · 1 · 15.0 · 15
TOGO · 1 · 15.0 · 15
IRAQ · 1 · 14.0 · 14
GUINEA-BISSAU · 1 · 12.0 · 12
ANGOLA · 1 · 11.0 · 11
CYPRUS · 1 · 8.0 · 8
MALI · 1 · 6.0 · 6
DPR KOREA · 1 · 5.0 · 5
MONTENEGRO · 1 · 5.0 · 5
GAMBIA · 1 · 2.0 · 2
AUSTRALIA · 1 · 1.0 · 1
AUSTRIA · 1 · 1.0 · 1
ECUADOR · 1 · 1.0 · 1
USA · 1 · 1.0 · 1

ROMANIA · 2 · 27.0 · 54
TURKEY · 2 · 25.5 · 51
SLOVENIA · 2 · 21.0 · 42
NIGERIA · 2 · 17.0 · 34
JAPAN · 2 · 16.0 · 32
ECUADOR · 2 · 14.5 · 29
DOMINICAN REPUBLIC · 2 · 9.5 · 19
GREECE · 2 · 9.0 · 18
BOSNIA AND HERZEGOVINA · 1 · 28.0 · 28
CONGO DR · 1 · 26.0 · 26
SWEDEN · 1 · 23.0 · 23
MARTINIQUE · 1 · 22.0 · 22
WALES · 1 · 19.0 · 19
ICELAND · 1 · 17.0 · 17
POLAND · 1 · 13.0 · 13
TUNISIA · 1 · 13.0 · 13
MALI · 1 · 11.0 · 11
RUSSIA · 1 · 11.0 · 11
ISRAEL · 1 · 9.0 · 9
QATAR · 1 · 9.0 · 9
BURKINA FASO · 1 · 7.0 · 7
AUSTRALIA · 1 · 2.0 · 2

175

Credits

The publishers would like to thank the following sources for their kind permission to reproduce the pictures in this book.

Getty Images: /AFP: 70; /Allsport: 58; /Odd Andersen/AFP: 96; /Matthew Ashton: 66; /Bentley Archive/Popperfoto: 8; /Gabriel Bouys/AFP: 166; /Tim Clayton/Corbis: 48, 97; /Philippe Desmazes/AFP: 170; /Denis Doyle: 58; /Stuart Franklin/Bongarts: 160; /Andreas Gebert/Anadolu Agency: 133; /Xavier Laine: 156; /Albert Llop/Anadolu Agency: 87; /Giuseppe Maffia/NurPhoto: 39; /Clive Mason: 152; /Jamie McDonald: 138; /Damien Meyer/AFP: 126; /Ryan Pierse/ FIFA: 168; /Popperfoto: 24, 28; /Manuel Queimadelos Alonso: 118; /Michael Regan: 100; /Clive Rose: 31; /Lukas Schulze/UEFA: 93; /Bob Thomas: 61, 88, 98; /VI-Images: 112

Offside Sports Photography: /L'Equipe: 54

PA Images: /Bruno Press: 44

Shutterstock: /Pix4Pix: 121

Every effort has been made to acknowledge correctly and contact the source and/or copyright holder of each picture and Carlton Books Limited apologizes for any unintentional errors or omissions that will be corrected in future editions of this book.